CLAIRE GORDON

The **Potential** Pack

Parents' Guide

CW00549809

CARROLL & BROWN PUBLISHERS LIMITED

For Craig Ainslie (1968-2003)

First published in 2004 in the United Kingdom by

Carroll & Brown Publishers Limited
20 Lonsdale Road London NW6 6RD

Art Editor Peggy Sadler
Illustrator Mark Buckingham
Photographer Jules Selmes

A CIP catalogue record for this pack is available from the British Library.

ISBN 1-903258-75-8

10987654321

Reproduced by RDC, Malaysia
Printed and bound in Singapore by Tien Wah Press

Contents

What is Multiple**Intelligence**?

Up until the 1980s, it was generally held that there was only one kind of intelligence, and that it was fixed at the same level at birth throughout our lives – our so-called IQ or intelligence quotient.

In 1983, Harvard education professor Howard Gardner published his groundbreaking book, *Frames of Mind: The Theory of Multiple Intelligence.* After extensive research, Gardner proposed that there are seven different types of intelligence, and that these can be developed, challenging the view that intelligence can be summed up in one IQ score.

Multiple intelligence theory is a positive and inclusive model of intelligence, which recognizes all the gifts we have, not just the 'academic' ones. It makes sense of the fact that there are many people whose success lies outside of the traditional intelligence framework, like concert pianists or Olympic athletes.

What are the multiple intelligences?

There are seven key areas, and in this book some of the intelligences have been broken down so that parents and children can explore them more fully.

To begin with, there are the two intelligences you are probably already familiar with, because they are measured in school as IQ:

Logical-Mathematical – the ability to use numbers effectively, and to deduce, reason and apply logic. In this book, these abilities are covered in Number Smart and Thinking Smart.
Linguistic – the capacity to use words effectively in speaking or writing. This is also known as Word Smart.

There are three specialist intelligences:
Musical – capability in perceiving, transforming, and expressing musical forms, also called Music Smart.
Spatial – skill in perceiving and manipulating objects or images, which is also known as Picture Smart.
Bodily-Kinesthetic – physical expertise in using one's body for expression or to produce things (Body Smart).

The last intelligences are the most unusual for an intelligence theory:
Intrapersonal – the ability to understand and manage one's own feelings (Self Smart), and
Interpersonal – the ability to understand and manage the feelings of others (People Smart).

Howard Gardner has always maintained that although he initially found seven intelligences that fitted his strict scientific criteria, there may be more. He has since recognized Naturalistic Intelligence (Nature Smart), for example. This is defined as the ability to recognize and classify plants, animals and natural phenomena.

What is Multiple Intelligence Theory?

Each person possesses all seven intelligences to some degree or another. We all, for example, have the ability to be musical but some of us can compose, while others just love the beat of the music.

There are many ways to be smart in each intelligence; for example, you can be linguistically intelligent because you are an amazing storyteller but not be able to read.

Most people can become reasonably competent in every intelligence, given the necessary encouragement and instruction. Multiple Intelligence Theory holds that you are not stuck with the intelligence profile you were born with. Once you understand your intelligence strengths, you can use them to your advantage in the quest for self-improvement and development.

Intelligences are always interacting with each other in complex ways, and do not exist in isolation. A professional footballer, for instance, needs his spatial and bodily-kinesthetic intelligences to coordinate and interact if he is to pass the ball accurately.

Implications

Multiple Intelligence Theory goes beyond a psychological profile of intellectual abilities. It recognizes that we all have strengths and weaknesses, but that by working on our weaknesses we can improve. One of the most positive aspects of the theory is its role in teaching and learning.

Some schools have embraced multiple intelligences as their philosophy, and children are taught topics in a way that appeals to their individual intelligence strengths. For example, if a class is learning about Guy Fawkes, the children might compose a song about him (musical intelligence), write a play about his life (linguistic intelligence), act it out (bodily-kinesthetic intelligence), or draw an annotated picture (spatial intelligence). You can help your children at home using the same formula.

To sum up, Multiple Intelligence Theory means that we are all smart in at least one way, that we can develop our intelligence, and that there is a framework for learning and developing that plays to our individual strengths. How smart is that!

Working with the **Tests**

It is increasingly common now for schools to use psychological tests as a way to find out more about students. Initially, testing may form part of the selection process, then it can help allocate children to appropriate classes, and later it may be used for monitoring progress.

Tests also can be used with children to promote self-understanding – and this is the purpose of this kit. You and your child may want to know why he or she finds some things easy and others difficult, whether a particular learning style might make it easier for your child to learn, and what your child's talents are so that they can be developed.

The tests and how they "work"
There are 34 separate tests, each produced as a card. There are approximately four tests of each intelligence. A "joker" card sorts the tests into their different categories.

If you glance through this book and the cards, you will notice that the tests vary in format and approach, as well as content. Some tests can be done with only a pencil and paper for writing answers, others require more in the way of materials. The answer structure varies,

too. Some tests have right and wrong answers, and you will calculate a score at the end of the test while others, particularly the people and self smart tests, act as springboards for discussions between you and your child, and you will need to interpret your child's responses based on your child's ability to think independently, his or her enjoyment of the task, and his or her understanding of the subject matter.

The tests have been designed as separate cards for a number of reasons. Firstly, separate cards make the tests seem less like an assessment, and more like a pack of fun things to do. Secondly, where tests do have correct or incorrect answers, the cleverer children out there will not be able to peek at the answers, or get distracted by flicking through the book. Finally, you can choose to let your child pick a card (from a pre-selected handful), and have some influence over the activity undertaken. Children who "buy in" to a test, are enthusiastic, interested, engaged, and will naturally perform better, so you will get a clearer and more accurate picture of their strengths.

At all times bear in mind that this kit has been designed as a development tool and should not be used to push your child to achieve a certain level or performance criteria. Just have fun spending time together!

good idea to start at the younger age range, to build your child's confidence and ensure that the concepts behind the tests are fully understood.

When you come to interpret your child's score or ability for a test, think about his or her performance as a whole. Are you confident your child understood the task completely? Did your child concentrate and really engage in what he or she was doing? Was your child tired or distracted? These are factors that can adversely affect performance. Most importantly, did your child enjoy it – people usually like the things they are good at.

Interpreting the tests

You will get a much broader picture of your child's strengths if you do all the tests in a chapter. Word smart, for example, has word and letter puzzles, and looks at written as well as spoken language. Within body smart, your child may be great at using his or her hands, but less coordinated at whole body movement. There are lots of ways to be smart in a particular area.

The majority of the tests are designed to be used with the full age range of 4-to-9-year-olds. However, the thinking-, word- and number-smart tests have been split into smaller age ranges to reflect the difference in ability between 4-to-6-years-olds and 7-to-9-year-olds. It's a

Using the parents' guide and record book

The parents' guide gives you the background for each type of intelligence and each specific test. It also provides guidance on administering and assessing each test and, sometimes, makes suggestions as to clues. The guide also explains how to extend some of the activities. It also provides boosting tips at the end of each test; these can be used both to stretch the child who has performed strongly as well as to give extra help to any child who needs it.

The record book is the ideal place to keep track of your child's results, the dates the activities were done, and to note any particular facility, skill to be improved, or interest.

What is Thinking**Smart**?

If you imagine your mind as a muscle, then, just as you use the muscles in your legs in various ways to walk, run or jump, so, too, can your brain be used for different purposes. Thinking smart is the ability to harness your thoughts and put them to these different uses.

There are several ways of thinking, and the exercises found in this chapter test the three main processes:

Logical thinking is the discipline of using step-by-step reasoning to see the patterns in a problem and find a rational solution to it. This involves considering possibilities, assessing information, and deciding on the most likely solution. In everyday life we use experience and knowledge to aid logical thinking.

Creative thinking is almost the opposite of logical thinking. Rather than finding just one solution to a problem, with creative thinking you generate as many solutions as possible, without appraising them. This gives your mind freedom to explore, rather than following a strict route. Thinking creatively may feel counter-intuitive, as we are taught to be logical from a young age.

Abstract thinking has similar principles to logical thinking, as they are both forms of reasoning. However, abstract thinking involves coding and decoding, and seeing patterns in symbols and shapes.

Developing thinking smart at home

If your child goes to nursery or school, you may feel that he spends the whole day thinking. However, the emphasis in schools is very much on logical thought, so you really can help your child by introducing him to the other types of thinking. Also, your child may not be aware that he is using logic to learn at school, so it is important to introduce the concept. The valuable skill of using logic to answer questions and solve problems will be the root of your child's learning.

You can introduce creative thinking as an early stage in logical thought. Encourage your child to spend time thinking creatively around a problem before he commits to an answer. That way your child will come up with the best possible solution.

Helping your child with the activities

The thinking-smart assessments have been designed to be fun, and to demonstrate the different thinking styles. Cognitive development is very much age related, so the logical tests have been divided into those for younger children (aged four to six) and slightly older children (aged seven to nine). True logical thinking doesn't really show itself until the age of seven.

Don't try to assess all the thinking smart tests in one session. Your child may be quite tired after each one because the tests require real concentration. The logical thinking activities will seem like school tests to your child, so only undertake these if he is in the right frame of mind. The abstract thinking and creative thinking cards will seem much more like games, and can be great for when he is bored or you have an hour to fill.

What to look for

Younger children often find it difficult to use reasoning, since they may only just be starting to think logically. The creative thinking tests will probably be the easiest to start with because younger children's fertile imaginations can act as a springboard into this type of activity.

Always remember that your role is to help your child develop reasoning, so use the clues if you need to, and be sure to focus on his understanding of the tasks rather than the eventual outcome.

Older children can now think logically, but to get the best out of them, present the tests as "puzzles", rather than as assessments. Children

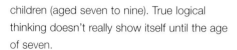

Whiz**Kid**

Bill Gates

William (Bill) H. Gates III was born on 28 October, 1955, and was programming computers at age 13, a sure sign of logical intelligence. At Harvard University, he developed a version of the programming language BASIC, demonstrating his abstract reasoning abilities with codes. In his junior year, Gates dropped out of Harvard to devote his energies full-time to Microsoft, a company he had started in 1975. His creative thinking led him to believe that the personal computer would be a valuable tool on every office desktop and in every home, so he began developing software for them. Today, Microsoft is the world's leading provider of software for personal computers.

of this age love the idea of secret codes, so your older child also should enjoy the abstract reasoning test.

First lessons in logic

The discipline of using step-by-step reasoning in order to find the best possible solution to a problem or sort through information is a valuable life skill. Logical thinking will help your child resolve disputes, quickly pick up new subjects in school, and make sense of the outside world.

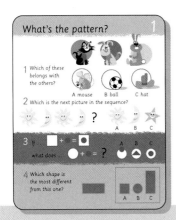

1 What's the pattern?

Sit down with your child and explain that she needs to look at the pictures carefully. Talk about the patterns you can see all around you, both visual (stripes on a T-shirt) and conceptual (apples and pears are both fruit). You may need to use the clues or point to the relevant part of the picture to keep your child's attention, but let her try first.

How did it go?

If your child got two or fewer answers correct, it is probably because children of this age are only just learning about "logic", and tend to be impulsive by nature! Encourage your child not to rush, and to talk through why she chose a particular answer. After the test, you can use the questions to teach her about recognizing patterns and problem solving. If your child got three or more answers correct, she is well on the way to being a logical thinker. You could use the test questions as a template for writing your own logic problems and improve her grasp of logic even further.

Boosting activities

■ Children love to collect things, and it's a great hobby because it helps them learn to sort and classify information. If your child doesn't already have a collection, encourage her to start one, maybe of coins, stamps or postcards – something that fascinates her. Talk about the different ways you could categorize the items, such as by country, size or colour, and then help your child put the items into the different groups.

■ Find some old magazines, and let your child browse through them. Decide on a category – for example things that are blue, or things that you can find at home – and cut out any pictures in that category. You could then make a collage by sticking the pictures on to a large sheet of paper.

Clues

1 They're all animals, aren't they?

2 Sun, moon, sun, moon … what comes next?

3 This is like a sum … if you add a square and the circle, you get a circle in the square.

4 A rectangle has straight sides, hasn't it?

Correct answers

1 **A** ▪ 2 **A** ▪ 3 **C** ▪ 4 **B**

Patterns and sequences

These puzzles are fun to practice and will not only improve your child's marks but also make it easier for him to perform well in many other types of tests. We can't prepare children for all of life's events, but the child who can think logically is better prepared to solve day-to-day problems as they arise.

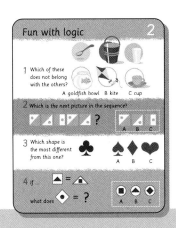

2   Fun with logic

These questions are similar to the logic tests older children encounter at school. They take the form of visual prompts which guide the user through patterns and sequences. Read through the instructions together and, if necessary, use the clues as pointers.

How did it go?

If your child got two or fewer correct answers, it was probably because he is still learning to think logically. But don't worry; a child's ability to apply logical reasoning improves all the time. To help your child develop reasoning skills, try the test for the younger age group, which will help him understand simple patterns and be a confidence booster.

Three or more correct answers indicate that your child is showing a talent for logical thinking that will be a real advantage at school and later in adult life. He probably enjoys school subjects such as maths and science.

Boosting activities

■ As well as helping to develop your child's ability to solve problems and improving social skills, many card games require logical thinking. Recommended card games include Rummy and Klondike (which can be played solo by your child or as a great family game for two or more players. It involves collecting and sorting cards by suit or number).

■ Play "What if?" by asking your child to talk through what he would do in response to an imaginary situation. You could ask, "What would you do if you got lost at the shops?" or "What would you do if you found a gold ring in the street?" When you know what your child's reaction would be, encourage him to think through the consequences of that choice.

Clues

1 They're all used for holding liquids, aren't they?

2 The dot changes places, doesn't it ... what comes next?

3 This shape has a curved top.

4 Now the triangle is on the outside.

Correct answers

1 **B** ▪ 2 **C** ▪ 3 **B** ▪ 4 **C**

Creative thinking

Thinking creatively involves widening your options when solving a problem rather than narrowing them down. This free-thinking exercise will help your child to apply imaginative solutions to practical problems – a crucial factor for success in future life.

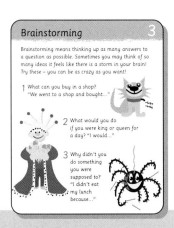

Brainstorming   3

Brainstorming means thinking up as many answers to a question as possible. Sometimes you may think of so many ideas it feels like there is a storm in your brain! Try these – you can be as crazy as you want!

1 What can you buy in a shop? "We went to a shop and bought..."

2 What would you do if you were king or queen for a day? "I would..."

3 Why didn't you do something you were supposed to? "I didn't eat my lunch because..."

3 Brainstorming

The point of this activity is to encourage your child to be as imaginative as possible. Brainstorming is useful for tackling a situation where unusual and new ideas, rather than obvious and boring ones, are needed. It is excellent for unlocking and loosening the thought processes. Younger children will probably need some prompting, so use the suggestions opposite to get your child started.

How did it go?

Did your child
- Understand the activity?
- Enjoy coming up with ideas?
- Seem able to produce lots of suggestions?
- Really get into the spirit of the activity?
- Demonstrate an increased interest in creative thinking after the activity?

If the answer is "yes" to three or more of these questions, then your child is clearly learning to use her brain with dexterity.

Boosting activities

■ Improve your child's ability to generate ideas by suggesting a subject and asking her to tell you about as many items or activities as possible that relate to it. For instance, you could ask your child about all the possible ways a person could travel to school, or to list all the places in the world that she could hide a favourite toy.

Suggestions

1 Animals ... Toys ... Bananas

2 Eat ice-cream for breakfast ... Not have a bath ... Go camping ...

3 A spider sat down beside me ... It disappeared when I picked up my fork ...The dog ate it ...

If the answer is "no" to three or more of these questions, then your child may not yet realize that creativity can be harnessed consciously. Children use their imaginations all the time in play, so your child's ability to think creatively is just waiting to be discovered and developed!

■ An important element in creative thinking is the ability to see the world in different ways to how you normally perceive it. You can help your child appreciate that there are many different ways of living or values in life by teaching her about other communities and cultures. Research a different religion together, visit your local Chinatown, or go out for a Thai, Indian, or Italian meal. Talk about how different people live.

Abstract reasoning

This type of thinking involves seeing patterns in symbols and shapes and decoding them. It enables children to understand that familiar things can be represented in different ways, which is essential when learning how to play a musical instrument or to speak a new language.

Secret messages   4

You can make your own secret messages by creating a code that only you and another person can understand. Write down all the letters of the alphabet, or just those letters in your name. Think of a different picture or symbol for all the letters.

Here's an example

I LOVE MOM

If your name was MOLLIE how would you write it in the code above?

Now try writing your own secret messages!

4   Secret messages

- You will need a pencil and some paper for this activity.

Your child should write the letters of the alphabet or her name on the paper, leaving space next to each letter. You can do this for a younger child. Ask your child to create a unique symbol next to each letter, and make a copy so that you both know which letter of the alphabet each symbol represents.

How did it go?

Did your child
- Understand the activity?
- Come up with the right solution for Mollie?
- Create her own code?
- Enjoy writing secret messages?
- Become more interested in codes after the activity?

If the answer is "yes" to three or more of these questions, then your child is demonstrating a great grasp of abstract concepts and the idea that codes can be created and interpreted by others.

Boosting activities

- Learn some words of an unfamiliar language and use them together. You could buy or borrow a simple phrasebook or a language learning tape for the car. This activity reinforces the idea that something may be represented by a different word but still have the same meaning.

- Go on a treasure hunt! Make a map of your home or garden and use symbols to represent the objects in it. Mark the treasure (a small gift, or sweets) with an "x" on the map. Give your child the map and see if she can interpret the symbols and find the treasure.

If the answer is "no" to three or more of these questions, then your child may find that thinking in abstract terms does not come naturally, and is probably more creatively minded. Try the boosting activities to encourage abstract reasoning in your child.

What is Word**Smart**?

Formally known as linguistic intelligence, word smart refers to the ability to communicate with and understand both written and spoken words. It breaks down into three components – communication, self-expression and word-power. Children who can use words easily and gracefully in written or verbal form have a great head start for adult life. After all, verbal communication is the main method of human interaction. You can help your child to become word smart by encouraging him to use spoken language in a variety of ways and for different purposes.

Studies suggest that children who are advanced in language development come from homes where they encounter a rich variety of spoken and written language. In an attempt to introduce a passion for language into your home, surround your child with lots of printed material like storybooks, posters and magazines. Be a good role model and show him what you like to read and why you enjoy it. Strive for greater interaction with your child when reading stories out loud. Choose a relatively short tale that will hold his undivided

attention. Stop and ask your child questions at key points. Using more "why" rather than "what" questions is a good way of teaching a child effective ways of self-expression and clear communication.

It is important for children to have someone to talk to in order to gain mastery over language, especially in the early years. Make sure that you and your child actively interact during any conversations that you have. Point out objects and people in your immediate environment, and discuss and categorize them.

With older children, discussing the variety of different languages spoken in the world might be useful. Find a map or an atlas and, with the help of your child, choose three countries that speak languages other than your own. Using either books from home, the library or by searching the Internet, research the equivalent words in each of these three languages for the following: "Hello", "Goodbye", "Please", "Thank you", and "My name is ..."

Helping your child with the activities

When your child does the tests in this section, encourage a 7- to 9-year-old to work independently with minimal guidance from you. Younger children will need more of a hands-on approach and greater encouragement. Remember that the majority of children love to talk, so what you as a parent are effectively evaluating is the manner and the diversity with which your child actually uses words, phrases, sentences and expressions, not his general level of talkativeness.

What to look for

Younger children will mostly be successful at carrying out the instructions so long as all that is required is the use of familiar vocabulary and a straightforward, factual style of verbal delivery.

Remember to give your child lots of praise – after it's been earned, of course – to build up confidence and reward his effort and enthusiasm. Words of encouragement nourish verbal communication skills.

Older children will really enjoy completing the projects in this pack and will obey instructions to the letter. A child's love of language or talent for verbal communication will be evident in his speech through the confident use of humour, a wide and varied vocabulary range, or verbal details that are put forward in memorable ways to really engage an audience.

Whiz**Kid**

Oprah Winfrey

Born on 29 January, 1954, in Kosciusko, Mississippi into a small local farming community, Oprah Winfrey's grandmother taught her how to read and nourished her love of public speaking. By the age of three, she was reading the Bible and reciting in church. Winfrey's career as a television talkshow host, actress and producer had already begun.

Spelling it out

Words, and the letters they contain, are the basic units of language, and word power is the ability to manipulate them confidently. If your child understands the different sounds each letter makes, the rules of sentence construction and is confident in using words, then she will find more complicated linguistic skills easier to acquire.

Letters and sounds   5

1 Write these sentences correctly
A is My green. coat
B dog run. A can

2 Fill in the missing letters:
A d_ck
B sh_e

3 Choose the
rhyming words
A red
B look
C took
D bed

4 Which of these
words are clothes
you can wear?
A hat B nap
C sock D bowl
E tick

5 Try these word sums
A d + ow + n = ?
B f + a + ll = ?

5 Letters and sounds

- Your child can respond verbally to you, or write the answers down, in which case you should have some paper and a pencil handy.

Sit down together, read through the instructions, and make sure your child understands the questions.

How did it go?

If your child got five or fewer correct answers, then she may only just be starting to learn about letters, their sounds, and how they make words. The key thing is to make words fun, so make up silly rhymes together, including as many quirky words as possible.

If your child got six or more correct answers, then she is demonstrating real word power potential, and probably enjoys reading and talking about letters and words. If she responded verbally, encourage the writing of answers so she becomes more familiar with the written aspect of language.

Boosting activities

■ Take the letter tiles from a Scrabble set, or write letters on small pieces of card, making sure you have lots of vowels (a, e, i, o, u) and common consonants (b, c, d, g, l, m, p, s, t). Put the letters in a small, non-transparent bag and let your child pull out three or four letters. Arrange them on a table, talk about the names and sounds of the letters, and see if she can make any words out of them – real or nonsense.

■ Children often feel real ownership of their names and the letters in them, so, using the letters in your child's name, go out somewhere together and see how many times she can spot the letters. For "Beth" you might find a "B" in a street name (BULKLEY AVE), an "E" on a shop door (EXIT), a "T" on a food packet (TEA), and an "H" in a department store (HELP DESK).

Clues

1   Look at the picture!

2   What are those pictures of?

3   Try saying these words aloud. Which ones sound the same?

4   What's a ... ? (Say each word in turn).

5   This is just like maths, but with letters instead of numbers.

Correct answers

1A **My coat is green.**

1B **A dog can run.**

2A **u** ▪ 2B **o**

3 **A/D and B/C**

4 **A and C**

5A **down** ▪ 5B **fall**

Getting wise to words

Word power advances rapidly with older children. They can focus less on individual letters and more on the words themselves, subtleties of meaning, irregular spellings and how smaller words can be used as building blocks for larger ones. Older children can combine the spoken word with the written word – word smart can now really take off.

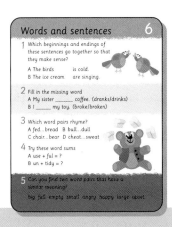

Words and sentences 6

1 Which beginnings and endings of these sentences go together so that they make sense?
A The birds   is cold.
B The ice cream   are singing.

2 Fill in the missing word
A My sister _____ coffee. (dranks/drinks)
B I _____ my toy. (broke/broken)

3 Which word pairs rhyme?
A fed...bread B bull...dull
C chair...bear D cheat...sweat

4 Try these word sums
A use + ful = ?
B un + tidy = ?

5 Can you find two word pairs that have a similar meaning?
big full empty small angry happy large upset

6 Words and sentences

- Your child should write the answers down, so have some pens and paper ready.

Sit down and relax with your child and read through the instructions together, making sure he understands them. Use the clues as prompts if he needs a little help.

How did it go?

If your child got five answers or fewer correct, he is probably still developing word-smart skills and is likely to be interacting with the world on a more physical or emotional level. He might benefit from playing more word games. Think about the questions your child had difficulty with and develop similar ones that he can practice.

If your child got six or more answers correct then he has developed excellent language skills. He has the ability to hear and read similarities and differences in words, which is a sure sign of word smart potential.

Boosting activities

■ Play word pyramids. Draw two squares at the top of a piece of paper, then three squares underneath it for the second row to form a triangle. Keep going until you have drawn a line of nine squares in the last row. Give the blank pyramid and a pencil to your child. He now fills every row with one word, placing a letter in each square. Have a dictionary at hand in case help is needed.

■ Buy a small notebook and help your child create his own joke book by writing in favourite gags. Riddles, puns, and "knock knock" jokes all involve a play on words. Here's a couple to start you off:

Q: Why couldn't the leopard escape from the zoo?
A: Because he kept getting spotted!

Have you heard the one about the duck, the deer and the skunk? They all walked into a restaurant. They ate their dinner, but the deer didn't have a buck, the skunk didn't have a scent, so they put it on the duck's bill!

Clues

1 Try saying the sentence to see if it makes sense.

2 Say the sentence aloud.

3 Try saying these words out loud. Which ones sound the same?

4 This is just like maths, but with letters instead of numbers.

5 Some of these words mean almost the same thing.

Correct answers

1A **The birds are singing.**

1B **The ice cream is cold.**

2A **drinks** ▪ 2B **broke**

3 **A and C**

4A **useful** ▪ 4B **untidy**

5 **large/big and angry/upset**

First steps in writing

You probably can't remember a time when you couldn't write, and it's difficult to appreciate the joy a child feels on finally being able to make a meaningful mark on a page that others can read. Younger children will need help so that they feel they are writing autonomously, even if they are just tracing letters or writing simple words.

All about me! 7

You are going to put together a scrapbook all about yourself, using writing to explain the pictures and other items you might use.

1 Think about how you would describe yourself and the things that are important to you. You might want to include your family, pets, school, holidays, likes and dislikes, hobbies, favourite things and friends.

2 Collect pictures, photos and anything you can stick in a scrapbook that describes you in some way.

3 Decide on the words that go with every picture, like "My brother loves cooking!" with a photo of him in the kitchen, or "My favourite football team is Liverpool!" with an old ticket.

4 Ask a parent for help with writing if you need to, but remember – YOU get to decide on what to say!

7 All about me!

- For this activity you will need a small scrapbook, pens and glue. You also may want a camera.

Help your child collect visual information to illustrate her life. This could be new or existing photos, old tickets for journeys or events, or pictures from magazines. Make sure the pictures cover a range of categories, such as family, holidays, hobbies or friends. Help your child paste the items in the scrapbook, grouping them as she wants, and leaving space around each one for a caption. Encourage your child to write as full a caption as possible by the appropriate picture. A younger child can trace her captions over your writing, or dictate the caption to you. As well as being a valuable exercise, the scrapbook will make a lovely memento.

Boosting activities

- Help your child create her own library. Have her choose ten favourite books and help her write the title and author of each one on a separate index card and stick the appropriate card to the inside of the book. Keep all the books in a box, and when your child wants to borrow a book, she can stamp the card using a small "stamper" (available from stationery shops). You can take it in turns to be the librarian and the reader and you could reinforce this activity with a trip to your local library.

- Include your child when you draw up your shopping list. She could trace over your writing, or you could help with spelling.

How did it go?

Did your child
- Understand the activity?
- Enjoy coming up with categories and pictures to illustrate her life?
- Find it easy to produce captions?
- Really get into the spirit of making the scrapbook?
- Demonstrate an increased interest in writing after the activity?

If the answer is "yes" to three or more of these questions, your child's language skills are well developed, and she is showing an aptitude for written language. This will become increasingly important when she starts school.

If the answer is "no" to three or more of these questions, your child is still developing her linguistic ability. Word-smart skills increase rapidly; you'll be surprised at how much progress your child can make in a very short time – there's a big difference in what a four-year-old and a six-year-old can achieve.

Creative writing

Once children are at school, they may feel that writing is a chore rather than a pleasure. You can awaken a love for writing in your child by helping her use it for self-expression. We all feel tremendous satisfaction in expressing ourselves, and it can be therapeutic for your child to put her feelings down on paper.

Something funny happened... 8

You are going to write a short story, called "Something funny happened on the way to school...". Here's some advice to get you started:

▷ The start... Always try to make the opening of a story interesting or exciting.

The characters... two or three characters (people or animals) are usually enough for a short story. Give them names, and describe what they look like. Try to show how they feel – write what they say and what they think.

▷ The setting... An exciting plot centres around an unexpected event, a crisis or a problem. Plans could go wrong – there could be an accident, or someone or something could get lost. Explain the result of the events.

The ending... Problems need to be sorted out by the end so the story is brought around "full circle". The final sentence is as important as the opening one. It usually sums up the story's theme or message.

8 Something funny happened...

■ Have some paper and pencils or pens ready.

Sit down and read through the instructions together, and make sure your child understands the activity. While you can do this activity together, some children may prefer to have a bit of personal space and to write it on their own.

How did it go?

Did your child
■ Understand the activity?
■ Enjoy coming up with characters and the plot?
■ Seem able to write with ease?
■ Really get into the spirit of it?
■ Demonstrate an increased interest in writing after the activity?

If the answer is "yes" to three or more of these questions, your child may well be a budding author! If she enjoyed the activity then you can easily adapt it for another day by varying the first line, so she can create a whole new story.

Boosting activities

■ Buy your child a diary or small notebook, and encourage her to keep a diary. Diaries don't have to be about innermost feelings – they can be a straightforward recounting of events, but do encourage your child to write every day, perhaps at the end of the day when she can record the details of her life in private.

■ Best-selling novelists say that they improve their own writing by reading that of other people. Reluctant readers often have not been exposed to a wide variety of fiction and non-fiction, so introduce your child to comics and children's magazines, both excellent introductions to the written word.

If the answer is "no" to three or more of these questions, think about which parts of the activity your child enjoyed most, and which proved more of a challenge. Maybe her talents lie in having a good imagination, or in telling a story out loud rather than writing it down.

The spoken word

While children often mispronounce a word or make the odd grammatical mistake, being "word smart" verbally has more to do with fluency and confidence with words. Learning one's own language is the same as learning to speak a foreign language; the only way to improve is to speak it as often as you can, in the presence of a native speaker who can correct you. As a parent, you have a similar role to the native speaker. You should always encourage your child to try to articulate things, even if he is unsure of finding the right words or expressions.

Try a talking game   9

1 **Under my bed**
The first player starts by saying, "I looked under my bed and found a..." and then makes up something he found, like "a puppy". The next player says, "I looked under my bed and found a puppy and ..." and then adds a second item, like "a tennis racket". Now take turns to add to the list. Start again when the list becomes too long!

2 **Cooperation story**
This game involves making up a story together. Start by saying "One day I was playing in the garden when ...". The next player adds to the story, ending with something exciting or unusual, like "an enormous flying saucer came out of the sky and ...". See how crazy and funny you can make the story!

3 **Watch your back!**
Cut out lots of pictures of items or animals from magazines or catalogues. Get another player to choose a picture, and stick it to your back with tape. You have to try to guess what it is. Ask for clues if you get stuck. Take turns to be the "guesser".

9   Try a talking game

These are three word games that your child can play with you, and/or a sibling or a friend; the first two games also are good when you are travelling or waiting somewhere. You could play the following variations with younger children:

Under my bed – the players don't have to remember the previous items, just make up something new each time.

Cooperation story – you can create the plot, leaving your child to add a few words rather than a whole sentence.

Watch your back! – you can let the child pick a picture and describe it to you without saying the name of it.

Boosting activities

- Make time to have a proper conversation with your child every day. This could be when he comes home from school, over supper, or when you are putting him to bed. Use open questions, such as, "What do you think we should do at the weekend?" or "What would be your ideal meal?" Try to avoid an interrogative question about what happened at school!

- Encourage your child to speak with visitors you have invited to your house so that he becomes used to communicating with different people. Visitors may have a strong accent or use unfamiliar words, so it is a good way of expanding your child's vocabulary as well as boosting his social skills.

- Other popular games, such as "I Spy" or "20 Questions" are great ways of passing the time constructively in the car, during intervals, or whenever you have spare time together.

How did it go?

Did your child
- Understand the activity?
- Enjoy playing the games?
- Seem able to speak with ease?
- Really get into the spirit of the activity?
- Demonstrate an increased vocabulary or enthusiasm for speaking aloud after the activity?

If the answer is "yes" to three or more of these questions, then your child has a strong grasp of verbal language, and you probably talk a lot together as a family. He is likely to enjoy using words and language, and can express himself well.

If the answer is "no" to three or more of these questions, then it could mean that your child found the games difficult to understand. Try some of the easier variations to build his confidence.

What is Number**Smart**?

Also known as numerical intelligence, this is the ability to use numbers confidently and successfully. Basic arithmetic is fundamental to number smart, but other key attributes are important too – such as the ability to reason and solve problems.

Number-smart children question, investigate and explore solutions to problems; demonstrate the ability to stick with a problem to find a solution; consider many different answers to a problem, and apply maths successfully to everyday situations, which is when it really comes alive for them. They also can use words, numbers or mathematical symbols to explain situations; to talk about how they arrived at an answer, and to listen to other people's ways of thinking, and, in addition to giving solutions to examples, they understand how maths works.

Encouraging numerical intelligence at home

The most supportive thing you can do is to have a positive attitude to maths yourself. Since mathematics has become increasingly important in many modern technology-based careers, it is vital that children learn maths at home as well as at school. Involve your children

in family decisions that use maths. Dividing up a pizza at mealtimes, counting change for a parking meter, or working out how much time he or she can spend at a friend's house are all useful activities your child can participate in.

Learning maths is a process of solving problems and applying what has been learned to new questions. In today's schools, the focus is on understanding the concepts and applying thinking skills to arrive at an answer.

Helping your child with the activities

The number-smart tests have been designed to be fun, and to promote mathematical

interaction between you and your child. The acquisition of maths is age-related, so the tests have been divided into those for younger children (aged four to six years) and slightly older children (aged seven to nine years).

The first two tests assess basic arithmetic, and will give you an indication of the learning stage your child has reached. Bear this in mind when you tackle the following two tests, which look at numerical reasoning – the use of maths in everyday life. Allow your child to work at his or her own pace, to take ownership of the activity and to enjoy it!

What to look for

Children aged four to six generally will be enthusiastic about the activities. The essence of numerical intelligence is feeling comfortable around numbers and taking pleasure in problem-solving using numbers. You should focus on exuberance rather than any error – it is your child's enthusiasm that will pay dividends in the years ahead.

Children aged seven to nine have well-developed maths skills, and can manipulate larger numbers with accuracy. They should be introduced to more sophisticated maths skills, such as estimating, quantifying, and presenting data in pictograms, bar charts or tables.

Whiz**Kid**

Srinivasa Aiyangar Ramunujan

Born in Southern India in 1887, Srinivasa was a great mathematics genius. All through his life, he was fascinated by numbers. At an early age, he studied trigonometry and pure mathematics on his own. He astounded his teachers with mathematical feats such as multiplying large numbers in his head. He later attended the Universities of Madras and then Cambridge, where he was elected fellow of Trinity College. Unfortunately his health was not good. He died aged 32, leaving behind his famous notebooks, through which modern mathematicians are still wading, trying to prove some of his theorems.

You should watch out for any loss of confidence with maths and address it immediately with lots of support and practice. Number-smart children have a strong self-belief in their ability to use numbers successfully, and this is developed by being stretched, learning from mistakes, and perseverance.

First steps in mental arithmetic

The foundation to good maths skills is mental arithmetic, and kids aged four to six years should be able to add and subtract numbers under ten with confidence. Children need to be able to add and subtract all the time in their daily lives, for example when keeping score in a rugby game, or when saving money for a special treat.

10 Party animals

Sit down with your child and ask her to look at the picture carefully. The theme of this card is parties, so you could talk about a birthday party she recently has been to. Read through the instructions together, and make sure your child understands the questions. With a young child, you may need to point to the relevant part of the picture to keep her focused.

How did it go?

If your child got two or fewer answers correct, then she is just learning that numbers correspond to amounts of objects. Children first learn to count by rote, (much as they learn a nursery rhyme by heart), but, by around the age of five, they gradually come to learn the significance of the numbers they are reciting. Encourage careful finger-pointing to actual objects when adding, and physically take away objects when subtracting.

Boosting activities

■ Buy some multi-coloured sweets, such as jelly beans or M&Ms. Ask your child to sort the sweets into groups of different colours, to estimate which pile has the most beans, and finally to count them to make sure. Sorting, estimating and counting are all key maths skills. You can extend this activity by rearranging the sweets and asking your child to re-count – many children will realize that the numbers remain the same. Finally, you could do some subtraction by eating the sweets!

■ Make up 11 cards, with the numbers 0 to 10 on them, plus three others for "+", "-", and "=". See how many different sums both you and your child can create by rearranging the cards. You can vary this activity to make it as easy or as difficult for her as you like.

Correct answers
1 **rabbit** ▪ 2 **12** ▪ 3 **7** ▪ 4 **6** ▪ 5 **6**

If your child got three or more answers correct, it reveals she has reached a crucial stage in maths, and now understands numbers in a more abstract way – that is, she will know that 2+2=4 without needing to have four objects in front of her.

Developing mental arithmetic

Basic number concepts (like bigger and smaller), and the ability to count forwards and backwards, are the foundations for understanding maths, and are normally in place by the time your child starts school. Children aged seven to nine years, however, can work with large numbers, and will benefit from lots of practice in adding and subtracting numbers up to 100.

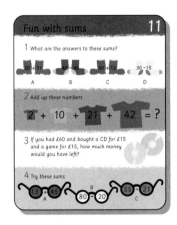

11 Fun with sums

- Older or very number-smart children may be able to do some of these sums in their heads, but make sure you have some scrap paper and a pencil ready as well.

Have you ever noticed that not many people in a supermarket, restaurant or department store will check their bills using a pencil and paper or even a hand-held calculator? That's because most of us do the maths in our heads, an ability often referred to as "mental arithmetic". This skill is vital in adult life, and once children start school, they can begin to develop it. Sit down with your child, read through the instructions together, and make sure she understands the questions.

Boosting activities

- Children usually find subtraction more difficult than addition. Examples of counting forwards (1,2,3,4...) are often heard, but children aren't as exposed to counting backwards (with the exception of space shuttle or rocket launching countdowns). Encourage your child to count backwards whenever you can. She could count from five down to zero when swimming lengths in the pool, or count the minutes left until bedtime. This exercise is even more effective if your child counts through the multiples of ten (for example, 22, 21, 20, 19, 18...).

- Bake some biscuits or brownies together. Cooking incorporates a variety of mathematical concepts, weighing, measuring, time, temperature, counting and volume. It also demonstrates clearly the value of maths to children – sometimes it can be hard for a child to see the point of all those sums!

Correct answers

1A **51** ▪ 1B **10** ▪ 1C **72** ▪ 1D **15**

2 **75**

3 **£30**

4A **58** ▪ 4B **60** ▪ 4C **34**

How did it go?

If your child got six or fewer correct answers, it is probably because it is a big learning jump from working with the numbers 0-20, to those up to 100. Your child is probably still getting used to the larger numbers, so it is important that you talk about the mistakes made – try asking how she arrived at the answers. The explanations will help you see where misunderstandings or lack of information played a part.

Seven or more correct answers indicate that your child is well on the way to being number smart, and probably enjoys maths problems. You can help develop this skill even further by encouraging her to try a problem even if it seems too difficult. Stretching children in this way speeds their development – however, you should always help if your child seems completely stuck.

Using maths in real life

Shopping is a great way to get your child to appreciate the importance of maths in real life – and to have fun with it. Budgeting, planning what to buy, counting money and checking change are all key maths skills.

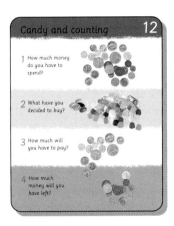

12 Candy and counting

- Set out a selection of sweets, each group with a price per item, and give your child some coins of all denominations.

Read through the questions on the card with your child and then let him "buy" what he likes. Offer to help with adding or subtracting. Let your child enjoy the sweets and any leftover change!

How did it go?

Did your child
- Understand the activity?
- Enjoy using maths in real life?
- Show confidence when using numbers?
- Really get into the spirit of the "shopping" trip?
- Demonstrate an increased interest in numbers after the activity?

If the answer is "yes" to three or more of these questions, then your child showed real number-smart potential.

If the answer is "no" to three or more of these questions, your child needs some help in becoming number smart. Try to find out what he didn't like about the activity and see if you can modify it.

Boosting activities

■ Ask for a clean French-fry container from your child's favourite fast-food chain. Take several yellow kitchen sponges and cut them into long strips – these will be the "French fries". Set up a table as the counter: your child will be the employee, while you will play the customer. Ask your child for a certain number of French fries and have him count them out. You could change your mind to let him practice subtraction.

■ Ask your child to trace his shoe on to a piece of paper and use it to measure distances around your home. Use it to find out how many steps it takes to get from one place to another. How far is it from his bed to the bathroom, or from the sink to the kitchen table?

Numbers in everyday life

Numbers are used in lots of different ways to provide us with essential information in everyday life – think of how hard it would be to find a house without its number or to buy new clothes without a price tag to guide you. The purpose of this activity is to help your child discover the significance and meaning of numbers in daily life.

Number hunt!   13

You are going to search for numbers. See how many you can find either inside your home or outdoors.

903258-43   3(
40
60

Write down all the different places you found numbers.
To get you started, look at the numbers on this card.
Can you work out where they came from and what they mean?

13 Number hunt!

- Your child will need a pencil and paper for this test.

Explore your house or neighbourhood with your child and encourage him to write down all the places numbers are found and what they mean. The examples shown on the card include a bar code, washing machine dial, clock radio, thermometer, ruler, calculator and clock. Outdoor examples could include buses or house numbers.

How did it go?

Did your child
- Understand the activity?
- Enjoy finding the numbers?
- Show confidence in interpreting numbers and numerical values?
- Really get into the spirit of finding numbers in everyday life?
- Demonstrate an increased interest in numbers after the activity?

If the answer is "yes" to three or more of these questions, then your child is showing real number-smart potential. Try extending this activity by presenting the findings in a table. Creating and understanding tabular numerical information is a great maths skill, and important for reading school or travel timetables.

Boosting activities

■ Keep a record of your child's height and weight. Let him read the scales and measure the height mark, and note it down in a special place. You even could draw a graph over time to show how he has grown.

■ Estimating is an important everyday skill and an excellent back-up when using calculators – we've all forgotten to add a number, or slipped a finger on the number pad. Ask your child to guess the number of sweets in a jar, the value of coins in your wallet, or the heaviest toy in his room.

If the answer is "no" to three or more of these questions, then your child may need more encouragement to develop his numerical skills. Talk about numbers whenever you can: those on a remote control or on sports shirts, or in addresses and telephone numbers. Ask your child why we use numbers in these situations.

What is Body**Smart**?

How you use your body – your control of it and your ability to use it skillfully in combination with other objects – is what's known as body smart. We often find it difficult to think of our bodies as "intelligent" because although we perform a vast and varied amount of tasks throughout the day, most are at a sub-conscious level. But our bodies don't just do their own thing as we walk, drive or reach for a product on a supermarket shelf. Our minds are coordinating all the movement.

Think about a world-class athlete running a marathon. She will have formulated a strategy for the race. She calculates speed as she runs, and knows when to slow down to avoid burnout. She is coordinating her muscles and breathing, and she has the physical fitness to run for hours. So a lot of brain power is involved! But body smart is not only about sport; other body-smart people include dancers, actors, painters and even dentists.

The tests in this chapter look at four main aspects of body smart:

Hand-eye coordination – the ability to use the hands precisely to control objects.
Whole-body coordination – the ability to coordinate the entire body's movements.
Balance – the ability to maintain and manage movement despite changes in environment.
Flexibility – the ability to undertake a wide variety of movement through the suppleness of the joints.

Encouraging physical intelligence at home

Not all of us will be brilliant athletes, or have the potential to earn a living as a performing artist, but we all need to be healthy, have strong muscles and joints and to avoid strain injuries in later life. Many of us have hobbies that involve using our hands, or get enjoyment from expressing ourselves artistically. These are pleasures we can pass on to our children.

As with many "smarts", the best thing you can do is to set a good example yourself and be active with your family. Sporty parents tend to naturally encourage their children to try out different activities, but if you aren't this way inclined you need to make an effort to add physical activity to your routine. Go on a picnic in the park and play ball games. Or do something creative together – model a clay bowl and paint it, or make necklaces and bracelets from beads and string. Get active and get creative!

Helping your child with the activities

The body-smart tasks are designed to give you an impression of your child's strengths and preferences: either whole-body control, part-body control, or the careful manipulation of objects. The activities also should be enjoyable, and will appeal to children regardless of their physical ability.

Give plenty of praise and try doing some of the activities yourself. Not only will you set a great example but children love seeing their parents make fools of themselves! Remember that you are trying to instil a lifelong interest in physical activity and body skills, so focus on having fun rather than criticizing performance. Body smart is one of those intelligences a child easily can improve – it just takes practice.

What to look for

Children aged four to six are likely to be clumsy because their coordination of brain and body isn't yet fully mature. They are more likely to do well on the flexibility tasks than the balance or whole-body coordination ones. Children this age can have very good hand-eye coordination, but any craft activities will still be a bit messy!

Seven- to nine-year-olds should be more fluent and controlled in their movements. Children this age often need to let off steam and love running around to get rid of excess energy! Look for signs that your child is particularly relishing an activity or an aspect of a task, as this is the best indicator of future promise. A child who enjoys something is more likely to practice it, and thus improve.

Whiz**Kid**

Venus and Serena Williams

The Williams sisters grew up in Los Angeles and both started playing tennis when they were just four years old, using old balls that they found. They were coached by their father, who taught himself to play from a book.

When Venus was nine and Serena was eight, they entered their first tennis tournament. Both girls reached the final and Venus beat her younger sister. Venus turned professional when she was 14, and quickly climbed the world ranking followed by her sister. The two made tennis history in 2001, when they became the first African-American sisters to play each other in a US Open final.

Hand-eye coordination

The following activities can determine how well your child is able to use his hands together with his eyes in order to accomplish a given task accurately. Your child will use this skill, for example, when learning to write, while playing tennis, or reaching for a glass of milk.

Cut, stick, construct 14

1 Make a model
Build a robot, dinosaur, or fairy-tale castle

2 Paint a picture
Create a portrait of your mum or dad or of yourself

3 Construct a collage
Paste pasta and dried peas and beans on paper to make a pattern

14 Cut, stick, construct

- **Make a model** Give your child some newspaper and cardboard, glue, adhesive tape and scissors. Have paints on hand to make the model look more realistic.

- **Paint a picture** Give your child paper and paints or colouring pens, pencils or crayons. Observe his skill in adding fine detail (like buttons on clothing or eyebrows), pointing out such details, if necessary.

- **Construct a collage** Offer your child a variety of dried beans, peas, and pasta and some glue, along with paper on which to form a picture.

Choose one or all of these projects for or with your child. If necessary, allow your child some practice time before observing and evaluating his hand-eye coordination. Focus on the synchronicity between hand and eye, rather than creative flair or sheer strength.

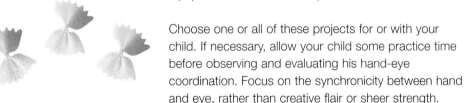

Boosting activities

■ Cut two lengths of string about 60 cm (2 feet) long. Twist one into any shape – it can be a random or a recognizable image. Get your child to replicate your design using his own piece of string. Take it in turns being the copier.

■ Place a scatter cushion on the floor about 1.5 m (5 feet) away from you. Have your child throw a beanbag (or a soft toy) at the cushion so that the beanbag (or toy) lands on or touches it.

How did it go?

Ages 4-6 Younger children should be able to use materials or handle objects with some dexterity, although the outcome won't be precise or even particularly tidy. Look out for your child's care and concentration during the task. Kinesthetic intelligence can be developed and refined throughout life, so having the opportunity to practice it while having fun is the most important thing!

Ages 7-9 Older children should be able to use materials or handle objects precisely and with skill. If your child really enjoyed doing the project, and seemed to find the task easy to complete, he has developed excellent hand-eye coordination.

Whole-body coordination

This is to do with how well you can use your mind to control your body – either one part, like using your hands to play a guitar, or your entire body, for when you run, climb or play football. And it's not just musicians or sports people who can use their whole bodies in clever ways – if your child shows good whole-body coordination potential, he might become a dancer or perform stunts.

Move your body   15

Actors use their entire bodies to communicate feelings to their audiences. You are going to mime (that means acting without speaking or making any sounds) some animals and people. See if your audience can guess what or who you are pretending to be ... but remember, no talking!

A dog: Get down on all fours, sniff around, wag your tail, and dig up a bone!

A musician playing the drums: Sit on a chair, and use your hands and feet to pretend you are playing a drum kit.

▶ A kangaroo: Pretend you are jumping along in the bush, eating some leaves, and looking after the joey (baby kangaroo) in your pouch.

A fisherman: Cast your line then act as if you are reeling in a huge fish. Then show your audience how big it is!

15 Move your body

This is a good way of encouraging your child to use his whole body for self-expression, and to think about how he should move to convey information. Your child will mime four things: a dog, drummer, kangaroo, and a fisherman. You are looking for whole-body coordination, rather than accurate acting skills, so make sure that – eventually – you guess correctly.

How did it go?

Did your child
- Understand the activity?
- Enjoy miming?
- Seem able to move with ease?
- Really get into the spirit of the activity?
- Demonstrate an increased interest in whole-body movement after the test?

If the answer is "yes" to three or more of these questions, it indicates your child is at ease with his body and able to control it well – a sure sign of being body smart. He probably enjoys sport, too.

Boosting activities

- Play "Blind Penny Hunt"—this works best with more than one player. Clear an open space in a room, removing any dangerous objects, and scatter pennies on the floor. Blindfold the children and give each one a paper bag. The players then crawl around the floor, feeling for pennies and collecting any they find in their bags. After five minutes, remove the blindfolds and check each bag – the winner is the child with the most pennies.

- Make time to exercise together as a family – go hiking, ride bikes, or swim regularly at your local pool. You could even have a family "disco" night, where you get dressed up, turn the lights down and dance around your living room to music. Get your child to work out a dance routine that you all learn and follow!

If the answer is "no" to three or more of these questions, remember that whole-body coordination is just one area of body smart. Your child's strengths may lie in using individual body parts such as his hands. Or, it may have been that the expressive nature of this task was inhibiting to him.

Flexibility

This refers to the amount of movement you have around your joints. Babies and children are extremely flexible, but muscle elasticity gradually decreases with age. Maintaining flexibility in children sets them on the path of healthy and safe joint movement, which is crucial for preventing injury in later life.

Yoga zoo 16

Yoga is an exercise that improves your flexibility, and gets your brain and body working together. It's also fun to do. Yoga postures often are named after animals, reflecting the different shapes your body can make. You are going to do two, the cat, and the cobra (a snake).

The Cat

Begin on your hands and knees. Keep your hands just in front of your shoulders, your legs about hip-width apart. Breathe in and let your spine dip down and your bottom tilt up. Gently lift your head and look straight ahead. Then, breathe out and round your back, pushing your bottom down, and curling your chin in towards your chest. Repeat as often as you like.

The Cobra

Lay on your stomach with your legs together and place your hands flat slightly in front of you. Breathe in, straighten your arms, and slowly raise your head and chest as high you can, making sure you look straight ahead. Breathe in and out several times and then lower yourself down. Repeat as often as you like.

16 Yoga zoo

Having muscle and joint flexibility is recognized as being both physically and medically beneficial. This exercise uses Yoga poses that kids will find enjoyable to perform. Yoga aims to connect the body and the mind by teaching you to be aware of your body as you move it into the different postures. This mental element makes it a great technique for developing body smart.

Practice these positions together, being careful not to push your child into any of the postures. Encourage your child to "listen" to her body and to stop when she has had enough.

Boosting activities

■ Write the name of ten different body parts (like "arm", "elbow", "hand", "leg", "knee", "foot", "stomach", "head", "ankle", and "bottom") on small pieces of paper, and put them in a bag. Ask your child to pick two pieces of paper from the bag at random and then try to make those parts of the body touch each other. Play together and you'll have a hilarious time trying to achieve some of the combinations!

■ Try limbo dancing. Position or hold a broom or mop handle horizontally so that your child has to bend backwards from the waist to move under the pole without touching it or losing her balance. Start at nose height, and gradually lower the pole. Add some steel drum music for extra fun!

How did it go?

Did your child
■ Understand the activity?
■ Enjoy forming the postures with you?
■ Seem able to get into the postures with ease?
■ Really get into the spirit of Yoga?
■ Demonstrate an increased interest in Yoga or flexibility after the activity?

If the answer is "yes" to three or more of these questions it shows your child has great flexibility. Your child's healthy joints will be a great asset as she matures. Make sure you incorporate flexibility activities into your child's everyday life to keep her joints supple.

If the answer is "no" to three or more of these questions, it could be because your child had difficulty understanding the task, rather than with her flexibility. If children can move easily, sit cross-legged, turn their bodies at the waist, or touch their toes, then they are displaying flexibility.

Balance

This is the ability to assume and maintain a position or activity, and to be able to adjust your centre of gravity to match your movement. It is much harder to remain steady while moving, yet our brains adjust to these changes automatically as we walk, jump or run. Shifting your centre of gravity on purpose is an important exercise in encouraging your brain and body to work together.

Balancing act   17

Here are some fun activities that will test your balance. Get your parent to help you set them up. You could do them on your own or with friends.

1 Circus tightrope
How far can you walk without "falling off"?

2 Sack race
How far can you jump without falling over?

3 Pirate treasure
Escape back to your "pirate ship" without dropping the treasure!

4 Crossing the river
Jump on the "rocks" so you don't fall in the water!

17 Balancing act

Make your own balance obstacle course from everyday items. If you do this activity indoors, make sure the surroundings are safe in case your child falls.

Choose from any or all of these ideas:
1 Circus tightrope – place a skipping rope, or a length of string on the floor in a straight line. Your child has to walk the length of the rope without "falling off".

How did it go?

Did your child
- Understand the activity?
- Enjoy the games?
- Seem able to maintain his balance while moving?

- Really get into the spirit of the activities?
- Demonstrate an increased awareness of balance after the test?

2 **Sack race** – give your child an old pillowcase, and mark the starting and finishing lines. Your child stands in his pillowcase at the starting line, and has to jump all the way to the finishing line without falling over.

3 **Pirate treasure** – fill a paper bag with small items such as coins, sweets or marbles. Have your child balance this "treasure" on his head, and then escape from you back to the "pirate ship" – this could be another room, up the stairs, or the end of the garden – without dropping the treasure.

4 **Crossing the river** – lay out five large pieces of paper in a path, and pretend they are rocks your child has to jump on. If your child touches the floor, he has fallen in the river.

Boosting activities

■ Get your child to help carry things for you, such as a light bag of groceries, or the dishes from the dining table, whenever possible. When we carry objects, our brain and body have to work together to adjust to the extra weight; this is great for developing body smart.

■ Encourage your child to try a new sport, especially one that has a focus on balance. You could go ice-skating, roller-blading, dry-hill skiing, trampolining or take classes in a martial art like judo. You'll have even more fun if it's something you can learn together.

If the answer is "yes" to three or more of these questions, then your child has great balance and is very body smart. The ability to maintain a centre of gravity, even when the body moves or is carrying something, will help him stay healthy and reduce the chances of injury.

If the answer is "no" to three or more of these questions, then your child probably found the tests difficult because balancing when moving or carrying a load takes a while to adjust to. Improving body balance is really a matter of practice, so encourage your child to have fun exploring it.

What is Picture**Smart**?

Can you imagine a cereal box? Now flip it around in your head so that you can see the top and back, and try to view it from different angles. That's the essence of picture smart – being able to see images and objects in your mind as clearly as if they were really in front of you! Being picture smart means you can read a map to find your way to an unfamiliar place, or take things apart and put them back together again with ease. You have a sense of objects and the space they inhabit.

The picture smart tasks look at four areas:
Spatial reasoning – the ability to think through visual problems and come up with the answers.
2D activities – the ability to visualize in two dimensions.
3D objects – the ability to mentally manipulate objects in three dimensions.
Mazes – the ability to orientate yourself in two dimensions to find a route through branching paths (a maze) or a single twisting and turning path (a labyrinth).

Encouraging spatial intelligence at home
Developing picture smart in your child involves getting her to focus on the visual side of things.

It can be particularly relaxing for a child who spends much of her time at school learning through words to spend time in the visual world. Some children with dyslexia have been found to be very picture smart.

You can help your child become more visually aware by starting a "picture-smart box" at home, which you can fill with a variety of stimulating materials and objects. Paper, pens, paints, glitter, glue and tissue paper are staple art materials. Modelling clay and beans, pasta or beads are ideal for making collages. You also can collect household packaging junk, like egg cartons, food boxes, and old magazines or comics for cutting out and inspiration. Construction toys such as Lego and wooden blocks are good, too. Turn off the TV and spend time together creating a picture or a model. Let your child take the lead.

Helping your child with the activities
Do explain to your child what picture smart means. You should focus on two dimensions with younger children and introduce three dimensions to older children. Use the analogy of the cereal box to explain the sort of thinking the tests will explore. Talk about how picture smart is used in everyday life, for instance in assembling a new toy, or reading a map, as

well as the sort of work people do who are picture smart. Architects, designers, engineers, artists and builders all use different aspects of picture smart to create things.

The first task, changing shapes, looks at spatial reasoning. It has a format similar to school tests, so don't attempt it if your child is tired. The "Smart art" and "Do it in 3D!" tests are art projects and are really fun, when you have sufficient time. The final test involves mazes and labyrinths, which children seem to love, and there are lots of ideas for extending the maze theme.

What to look for

Younger children particularly will enjoy the art activities but they may find the spatial reasoning tests difficult. Picture smart is quite conceptual, so it may be difficult for younger children to understand some of the activities. Older children should be able to understand all the projects, but may have preconceptions formed at school that they can't draw, or aren't good at art. Build up your child's confidence – everyone is picture smart in at least one way, you just need to find it.

For all children, focus on the visual and spatial element of the activities. You shouldn't be too concerned about the neatness of

drawing or the mess that may ensue with making things. Ask yourself whether your child seems to have a clear vision of what she is setting out to achieve.

WhizKid

Pablo Picasso

The son of an academic painter, Pablo Picasso was born in 1881 in Malaga, Spain. He began to draw at an early age and at the age of eight, produced his first oil painting "The Picador". In 1895, he moved with his family to Barcelona and studied at La Lonja, the academy of fine arts. His first exhibition took place in 1900. Picasso's "picture smart" abilties encompassed at least three dimensions: he collaborated on ballet and theatrical productions and he was a proficient sculptor. He produced a prolific amount of work including paintings, drawings, prints, ceramics and sculpture.

Spatial reasoning

In the same way as we use reasoning to think through problems in thinking smart, we can reason with shapes and space, which is known as spatial reasoning. This is the ability to imagine shapes in our mind, and how they can be moved or transformed. Shapes can be in two or three dimensions, but it is generally harder to manipulate images in 3D.

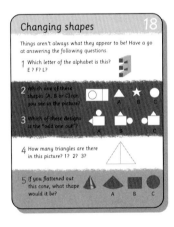

18 Changing shapes

Sit down with your child and explain to her that she needs to look at the pictures carefully. Talk about how shapes can look like different things if they are seen from different angles – for instance, a banana can look like a bridge if it's on its side, or like a crescent moon if you hold it upright. Read through the instructions together, and make sure she understands the questions. With a younger child, you may need to point to the relevant part of the picture to keep her attention, or to use the clues.

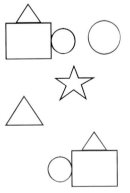

Clues

1   The letter might be back-to-front

2   The shape will be exactly the same in the picture

3   Imagine turning the shapes around in your head

4   The triangles might be different sizes

5   Imagine if you pressed the sides together

Boosting activities

■ Play games together that have a visual element in 2D or 3D, like tic-tac-toe, checkers or chess. These games help develop thinking smart as well as picture smart.

■ Make your own jigsaw puzzles by sticking an image your child likes, such as a pop star or cartoon character, on to a backing card, and then cutting out random shapes. You could do this activity together and make each other puzzles to try to solve.

How did it go?

Three or more correct answers show that your child is showing a gift for spatial reasoning, and probably enjoys playing games with a strong visual element. Encourage her to maximize this ability by using visual aids when learning.

Two or fewer correct answers indicate that your child is likely to be younger, since an awareness of perspective comes with life experience. Everyone is picture smart in some way, so your child's strengths may lie in the creative arts – or she may be a budding inventor!

Correct answers
1 E ▪ 2 C ▪ 3 A ▪ 4 3 ▪ 5 A

Visualizing in two dimensions

Some people, such as artists, graphic designers, illustrators and photographers, have a specific talent for creating and manipulating two-dimensional, flat images. Children with this talent are drawn to visual stimuli. Many make better sense of information by drawing an ideas map while others may enjoy making art like cartoons, sketches or watercolours. Others get pleasure from looking at art and love trips to galleries and museums.

Smart art   19

Try doing one or all of these art projects:

1 Patterns in nature
Collect examples of differently shaped and patterned items – shells, feathers, leaves, pinecones, flowers or tree barks. Present your collection on a tray, arranging your pieces carefully. Explain your collection to a grown-up.

2 Face painting
First, plan what you will paint on scrap paper – for example, you could be a butterfly, a clown, a tiger or a super hero. Stand in front of a mirror and draw on your face using suitable paints, according to your plan. You could even paint your mum's face!

3 Seeing things differently
Pick a small object, like a strawberry, button or a bottle top. Draw it with a pencil. Look at the object again using a magnifying glass, and draw what you can see. Similarly, draw a distant object then look at it using binoculars or a telescope. How different do things look close up?

19 Smart art

- **Patterns in nature** You will need a tray or large flat surface on which your child can present her collection.

- **Face Painting** You will need face paints, brushes, scrap paper, a pencil and a mirror.

- **Seeing things differently** You will need a magnifying glass and binoculars or a telescope.

Creating pictures with paper and art materials is something most children enjoy. Explain these tasks to your child and let her decide which one to create. Focus on your child's visual interpretation of each task rather than her skill or neatness.

Boosting activities

- Give your child a notebook for doodling in. Doodling promotes important subconscious thinking, and she may get new ideas or inspiration from looking back at previous drawings and sketches.

- Have a picture conversation. Ask your child a question like "What shall we have for dinner?" or "What shall we do today?" Your child then draws her response (say, a pizza). You then draw something in return (like a piece of pepperoni, a tomato, or some mushrooms) to find out what toppings she would like, and so on.

How did it go?

Did your child
- Understand the activity?
- Enjoy presenting what she saw?
- Seem able to creatively interpret what she saw?
- Get into the spirit of the activity?
- Demonstrate an increased interest in pictures, photographs or art after the exercise?

If the answer is "yes" to three or more of these questions, then your child is definitely picture smart, and is able to express herself well in two dimensions. Try test 20, "Do it in 3D!", to see if she has a flair for that, too.

If the answer is "no" to three or more of these questions, it could be because these tests are on the creative side, and your child might be picture smart in terms of appreciation rather than creativity. Learn about famous paintings together, or try making a collage from recycled materials.

Working in three dimensions

One of the key elements of picture smart is the ability to think about space – both objects in space and the space around you. This type of thinking calls on the ability to imagine three-dimensional objects in your head, and then to move around them in your mind and "see" them from different angles. Children who can do this may not be aware that they have this ability, and not all picture-smart people are able to think in three dimensions.

Do it in 3D! 20

Here are two ideas to transform your bedroom

1 Mobile magic
It's easy to use wire hangers and decorated paper cutouts or your own special objects to make a mobile. Think about how the mobile will look from every angle, including from below. Imagine it finished in your head, and draw a plan to remind yourself of how you want it to look. Will it have a theme, like the weather, sport or the planets, or will you choose objects that match your room's colour scheme? Use thread to fix each object to the hangers.

2 Bedroom remix
To give your bedroom a new look, rearrange the furniture. Imagine where you could move the items, thinking about the space you need to work or play, and the location of the door and windows. Draw a plan of your room, and cut out shapes to scale to represent your bed, storage, desk, chairs and so on. When you decide on your final plan, check it with a parent, and get his/her help to move things around the way you want them.

20 Do it in 3D!

- **Mobile magic** You will need paper and pencil, wire hangers, pliers, thread and your child's cutouts or his selection of objects.

- **Bedroom remix** You will need some graph paper, a pencil, a tape measure, a ruler and scissors.

Most children are very territorial about their bedrooms, so here's a chance for your child to express his individuality through it, and get picture smart at the same time. Choose one or both of these projects for or with your child – "Mobile magic" may be more appropriate for younger children, while "Bedroom remix" is better for older children. You will need to supervise your child for safety reasons, but try not to intervene in the creative process. Focus on the 3D element of each task rather than the appearance or suitability of the outcome!

Boosting activities

■ Make a papier-mâché head with your child by building up layers of newspaper strips dipped in a glue solution on to an inflated balloon. Leave the paper to dry, then decorate the "head" by painting on a face and adding yarn for hair.

■ Help your child to take apart an old tissue box carefully until it's a flat piece of cardboard. Then see if he can remake it using adhesive tape or glue. Seeing something in 3D, then 2D, then back to 3D again really demonstrates what picture smart is all about.

How did it go?

Did your child
■ Understand the activity?
■ Enjoy coming up with ideas and plans?
■ Seem able to imagine the outcome in 3D?
■ Really get into the spirit of the activity?
■ Demonstrate an increased interest in space and three-dimensional images after the activity?

If the answer is "yes" to three or more of these questions, then your child has a talent for thinking in three dimensions, which is a special kind of picture smart. Encourage your child to switch between 2D and 3D by drawing a 2D plan before he embarks on a 3D project.

If the answer is "no" to three or more of these questions, then it could be your child is younger, or he may be more comfortable working in two dimensions. Three-dimensional thinking tends to be something you either can or can't do, and lots of us find it difficult!

Labyrinths and mazes

Picture smart is about thinking in pictures and imagining objects in space. A fun way to explore this is to solve mazes. Mazes are puzzles made out of paths. They have a single destination but a number of dead ends in which you can get stuck. The oldest form of maze is the labyrinth, which has only one path and a central destination.

Amazing mazes   21

You are going to try and find your way out of two mazes.

"Enter" this maze at the arrow. See if you can "get out" without making any wrong turns!

With this maze, you also "enter" at the arrow but you want to end up in the centre.

21 Amazing mazes

Sit down with your child and the mazes – you could photocopy the card if you don't want your child to write on it. Emphasize the basic rule of mazes – you have to enter where the arrow shows you and find your way out or to the centre without crossing a line. You could extend the activity by talking about the difference between mazes and labyrinths.

How did it go?

Did your child
- Understand the activity?
- Enjoy trying to reach the end or centre of the maze?
- Seem able to follow the right path with ease?
- Get into the spirit of the activity?
- Demonstrate an increased interest in mazes or labyrinths after the activity?

If the answer is "yes" to three or more of these questions, then your child is skillfully combining 2D picture smart with elements of thinking smart, as he mentally anticipates dead ends. The ability to plan ahead and predict problems before they actually arise is valuable in adult life.

Boosting activities

- Get your child to design his own maze, using a sheet of graph or grid paper. Trace a 30.5 x 30.5 cm (12 x 12 in) box, use a pencil to sketch the route and the "dead ends", add the "walls" in pen, and then erase the pencil lines. If this activity really arouses an interest in mazes, check out the internet for web sites with online mazes and labyrinths.

- Pay a visit to a maze. Walking around a maze is a completely different experience to solving one on paper. Mazes can be made of hedges, brick walls and mirrors.

If the answer is "no" to three or more of these questions, it may be because your child is younger, or he may prefer not to work in two dimensions. Some picture-smart people actually prefer working in 3D because it is more lifelike, so try some 3D activities together, like modelling or sculpting.

What is Music**Smart**?

This is the ability to perceive, create and express music in all its forms. Musical intelligence develops very early, and a parent's voice or lullaby soothes even tiny babies. Toddlers often make up tunes, and love exciting songs.

Music smart can be "top-down", as in having an empathic and intuitive appreciation of music, personified in someone who is uplifted and inspired by musical notes and beats. It also can be "bottom-up", as in having an analytical and technical understanding of music, possessed by those who compose and perform music to high standards.

Making music calls on a number of other intelligences, too. Counting beats and learning about the structure of music depends on number- and thinking-smart skills, and you are coordinating your body in order to produce notes, using body-smart abilities. Music is a powerful method of communicating with others, literally and emotionally, so music smart can also help with people-smart skills.

Types of music smart

The tests in this chapter look at four main aspects of music smart:

Pitch – the ability to detect sounds on a musical scale, from high to low notes.

Rhythm – the ability to feel and produce the beat of music, used to measure time throughout a musical piece.

Listening to music – the ability to appreciate and understand music.

Making music – the ability to generate music using the voice or an instrument.

Encouraging musical intelligence at home

Children love music and even pre-crawling babies will sit and "bob" to a rhythm. Music is a safe environment for expressing feelings and emotions that are difficult for children to talk about, so it should be encouraged as an emotional outlet. A successful rendition of a song or musical piece gives children a wonderful sense of achievement and raised self-esteem. Playing or singing in a group helps children's social skills, as they mix with others outside of their established network of friends.

There are lots of ways you can encourage music smart at home, some need resources, others – such as singing – don't.

If your child has the opportunity to play an instrument at school, then encourage him to take it, and try to extend playing opportunities by finding out about local orchestras and bands he could take part in. If your child enjoys singing, he may be able to join a church or school choir.

Helping your child with the tests

The first two activities assess the main elements of music – pitch and rhythm. Having gauged your child's innate ability with these skills, you can have some fun listening to and making music in the next two tests.

A love of music is something we are all born with, but somewhere along the line we may tag ourselves with labels, such as "no good at singing" or "can't read music". If your child seems to be wearing one of these tags, you will need to build up his confidence to shake it off. Start by introducing music as fun before you attempt any of the tests – children need to be enjoying themselves before they reveal their talents to you.

What to look for

Children aged four to six are likely to enjoy all of the activities, but may have difficulty understanding the concepts of pitch and rhythm. Spend some time on pitch and rhythm if you feel your child would benefit from it.

Older children should be familiar with musical concepts, since they are taught in most schools. A child with exceptional musical abilities will find the tests quite easy, and will really relish doing them. If music plays a major part in your child's life, if he makes up songs, hums while completing tasks or remembers melodies easily, the chances are he is music smart.

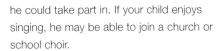

Whiz**Kid**

Wolfgang Amadeus Mozart
Born in Salzburg, Germany, in 1756, Wolfgang Amadeus Mozardt was an exceptional music-smart prodigy. He played the violin at three, and composed at five. He made his first pubic appearance at age six, in a harpsichord and piano concert tour of Munich and Vienna. One year later (1763), his first published composition was distributed in Paris. Mozart became Konzertmeister (at age 13) to the Archbishop of Salzburg. He possessed perfect pitch, and at age 14, he heard *Allegri's Miserere* at the Sistine Chapel and wrote down the score after one hearing. He produced a vast quantity of work but died at the age of 35.

Pitch

When a musical instrument is played it causes the air around it to vibrate. Our ears pick up these vibrations, and our brain interprets them as sound. If the vibration is steady, we hear it as a musical note. If it vibrates quickly, we hear a high note or pitch; if it vibrates slowly, we hear a low note or pitch. Recognizing the differences in pitch is an important part of being music smart. Some people are "tone deaf", in that they cannot reproduce or tell the difference between notes.

Pitch it right   22

Musical pitch is about what "note" a sound is – high or low. You are going to play a game where you have to guess whether two notes are the same or different.

1 Fill three glasses with different amounts of water.

2 Turn your back so you can't see the glasses and ask an adult to play one "note" followed by another.

3 Say whether you think the note is the same or different.

22 Pitch it right

- You will need three drinking glasses, some water and a small spoon.

Explain to your child that you are going to play a guessing game with musical notes. Your child should fill one glass with a small amount of water, the second so it is about half full, and the third glass so the water almost reaches the top. You may have to help small children. When your child is seated with his back to the glasses, strike the rim of one glass with your spoon to produce a target note. Then three seconds later, play another – either the same note, or one of the other glasses. Ask your child to tell you if the note was the same or different. Repeat until he has guessed whether five notes are the same or different.

Boosting activities

■ Accompanied by your child, find five different water vessels around the house, and fill each with some water. You could choose a jug, a vase or even a bucket. Ask him to strike the rim of each one with a spoon, and then to arrange them in order of pitch, from the lowest to the highest. You can extend this activity by asking your child to try to sing the note that each vessel produces as it is struck.

■ Play "Name that Tune" together. Take turns to hum or guess a tune to a well-known nursery or folk song – try "She'll be Coming Round the Mountain", "Three Blind Mice", or "Rudolph the Red-Nosed Reindeer".

If you have a piano or keyboard, you can do the same activity while playing the notes.

How did it go?

Three or more correct answers reveal your child has excellent pitch, and is probably already demonstrating an affinity for music through singing, playing an instrument, composing or listening to music. Your child may go on to develop perfect pitch.

Two or fewer correct answers indicate that he has average pitch, and probably found it difficult to hear subtle differences between the notes. While pitch is an important aspect of music smart, there are lots of other ways to be musically intelligent.

Rhythm and rhyme

Rhythm is the beat or pulse of a piece of music. If you find yourself swaying or tapping your feet to a song you love then your body is sensing and responding to its rhythm. Just as rhythm and pitch are the essence of music, so is a feeling for rhythm central to being music smart. Rhymes produce "catchy" lyrics!

Keep to the beat! 23

It can be fun making up new words, or lyrics, to well-known tunes. Try writing a new song to the tune of "Frère Jacques" (also known as "Are you sleeping, Brother John?"). Think about the number of beats in the rhythm, and remember that the words at the end of the lines should rhyme.

You can write about anything – your favourite sports star "John plays football ..." or something you like eating, "I love ice-cream ..." – whatever you like!

Here's an example:
"I hear thunder,
I hear thunder,
Can you too?
Can you too?
Pitter patter rain drops,
Pitter patter rain drops,
I'm wet through,
So are you!"

23 Keep to the beat!

Your child is going to write some new lyrics for the well-known nursery rhyme tune, "Frère Jacques". Ask her to chose words that reflect the rhythm of the tune, express an idea, and rhyme at the end of the appropriate lines. Help your child listen for the syllables in words, as each syllable is a separate beat.

How did it go?

Did your child
- Understand the activity?
- Enjoy coming up with lyrics to reflect her interests or ideas?
- Understand the rhythm and rhymes of the tune?

- Really get into the spirit of the activity?
- Demonstrate an increased interest in rhythm and rhyme after the activity?

Boosting activities

■ Most classical Western music has very ordered and measured rhythm: the lengths of individual notes are exact multiples or subdivisions of each other. "American" music has two separate rhythms, one for the drums and another for vocals. African music is known for its polyrhythms, which are many different rhythms that are played at the same time. Listen together to music from other cultures so you can pick out the different rhythms.

■ Using a tape recorder, help your child make recordings of everyday sounds with distinctive rhythms. Around your home you could listen to the sound of your washing machine or the phone ringing, and while you're outdoors, explore the sounds of birdsong, street repairs, or a train clattering across tracks.

If the answer is "yes" to three or more of these questions, then your child's sense of rhythm is well developed, and she is likely to enjoy dancing and clapping to the beat. A great sense of rhythm means great music-smart ability!

If the answer is "no" to three or more of these questions, then your child may not yet have discovered rhythm. You can encourage her by dancing or clapping along together to some music. Remember, rhythm can be very sociable!

Listening to music

Most music is written to express or invoke an emotion or feeling, and this is achieved through both the melody and the lyrics. Therefore, music smart has close links with self smart, and is a safe and personal vehicle for adults and children alike to consider thoughts and emotions. This exercise will help your child understand music's emotional aspects, as well as encouraging active listening to and enjoyment of music, both of which are important elements in being music smart.

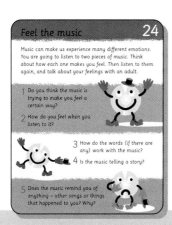

Feel the music   24

Music can make us experience many different emotions. You are going to listen to two pieces of music. Think about how each one makes you feel. Then listen to them again, and talk about your feelings with an adult.

1 Do you think the music is trying to make you feel a certain way?

2 How do you feel when you listen to it?

3 How do the words (if there are any) work with the music?

4 Is the music telling a story?

5 Does the music remind you of anything – other songs or things that happened to you? Why?

24 Feel the music

Set aside some time, maybe at the end of the day, when your child is likely to sit quietly. Listen together in silence to two contrasting tracks of music – one happy and uplifting, the other somber and sad. Then listen again, and afterwards talk about the emotions each track conveys.

How did it go?

Did your child
- Understand the activity?
- Enjoy listening to the music and talking about it with you?
- Seem able to describe the pieces accurately?

- Really get into the spirit of the activity?
- Demonstrate an increased interest in listening to music after the activity?

Music suggestions

Classical—from Gustav Holst's *The Planets Suite*: "Jupiter, The Bringer of Jollity" (happy) and "Mars, The Bringer of War" (sad)

Contemporary—Simon and Garfunkel's "The 59th Street Bridge Song (Feelin' Groovy)" (happy) and Elton John's "Candle in the Wind" (sad). Where pieces have lyrics, you can focus on those too.

Boosting activities

■ Expose your child to various kinds of music. Pick out a few examples of different genres of music from your own collection – jazz, pop, hip-hop, dance, classical, country, gospel, reggae or rock. Play some tracks to illustrate these music types and talk about what your child likes and doesn't like, and why.

■ Take your child to hear live music. Watch musicians express themselves through singing or playing. There is often free live music at fairs, festivals, parks or local schools.

If the answer is "yes" to three or more of these questions, then your child is great at actively listening to music – a sure sign of music smart, and an ability that will give him great pleasure in adult life.

If the answer is "no" to three or more of these questions it is probably because young children love music for music's sake, not particularly as a form of communication. Encourage this basic love, because a deeper appreciation of music will follow.

Making music

Singing or playing a musical instrument is probably the most evident way of being music smart, and these are the skills that come to mind when we think of musical intelligence. If your child already plays an instrument, or sings in the school choir, you'll know if she is "musical" in some way. But children who sing along to the radio, or drum their hands on the table, are also showing their ability to make music.

Rubber-band violin   25

You are going to make a simple "violin" and "bow".

1 Take an empty tissue box and place five rubber bands on the box so that they cross the opening.

2 Make your bow by stretching a rubber band over a pencil, from the eraser end to the tip, which should not be sharpened.

3 Now play your violin:

▸ Play each band with your bow. Do they all sound the same or are there differences?

▸ Pluck each band with your fingers. Does it sound different to using your bow?

▸ Experiment using rubber bands of different lengths and thicknesses on your violin. What are the differences in sound?

▸ Press your finger down on one band on top of the tissue box. What happens to the note the band produces?

▸ Play a tune!

25   Rubber-band violin

■ Gather together a tissue box, six rubber bands and a pencil, and sit together at a table. There should be no background noise.

Once your child has made the violin and bow, see that she explores the sounds made with the bow and by plucking the "strings". Focus on the musical aspects of this activity rather than your child's craft skills.

How did it go?

Did your child
- Understand the activity?
- Enjoy making sounds with the violin and bow?
- Seem able to produce notes, or even a tune?

- Really get into the spirit of the activity?
- Demonstrate an increased interest in making music after the activity?

Boosting activities

■ Your child needs to hear music to be able to play or create it. Sing along to music in the car, or listen to it instead of watching the TV. Let your child choose the CD. Music is also thought to help stimulate thinking, concentration, and memory.

■ Try making other musical instruments such as a drum from a bucket or flower pot, a rattle from a plastic pot filled with beans, or a horn from blowing across the top of an empty bottle. You could have a "jamming session" at home, with every member of your family playing together!

If the answer is "yes" to three or more of these questions, then your child's music-making abilities are a definite indication of music smart. You might want to develop this skill by helping your child to play music with others in a group or orchestra.

If the answer is "no" to three or more of the these questions, then it could indicate your child may not have discovered music making for herself yet, or it could mean her music-smart talents simply lie in another direction.

What is People**Smart**?

This ability helps us understand other people and their moods, motivations and intentions. It enables us to tune in to others, to empathize with them, to communicate clearly with them emotionally, to inspire them and to understand our relationships with them.

Children who are people smart genuinely like others, and tend to have a wide variety of friendships. They might be good at resolving conflicts, or are natural leaders. They are good at "reading" people, pick up emotional vibes easily and accurately, and reach out to those in need such as shy kids, or the less popular at school. In turn, they are easy people to be around, and sought after as play partners.

There are four people-smart tests; each covers one of the main skills in emotional intelligence:

Communication of emotions – understanding how people use their voice and sometimes gestures when they feel different emotions.

Conflict resolution – the ability to problem-solve and negotiate satisfactory solutions to relationship problems.

Forming and sustaining friendships – the ability to make new friends and enable existing friendships to thrive.

Coping with social setbacks – the ability to remain optimistic in the face of social rejection, and to speculate positively on reasons for the setback.

Encouraging emotional intelligence

Healthy friendships are a crucial part of childhood, and vital to your child's healthy development. Through friends, your child is learning how to get along with people, to understand his and others' emotions, to negotiate, cooperate, and compromise. You can help your child by expanding his circle of friends: invite a new child to play, or encourage your child to join a club based on his interests. Teach your child to be assertive, to let others know that he wants to play, or that his feelings are hurt, or that he doesn't like it when another child pushes him.

Talk with your child about what makes a good friend. Does he see, through your life, that he can be friends with anyone he chooses?

Helping your child with the activities

These tests require interaction between you and your child, by their very nature. The tests have been designed to encourage an open discussion between you. There are no right or wrong answers. It's very important that you approach the tests calmly and neutrally, to encourage your child to talk openly about his feelings and friendships. Make sure your child is "in the mood", and don't push for answers if your child has clearly had enough. Respect his privacy and try again another day.

It is possible that during a test, your child may choose to reveal something you weren't expecting. If anything he says worries you, discontinue the test, and use the opportunity to probe gently. Don't lose your cool; take time out to consider the best course of action.

What to look for

Children aged 4–6 tend to have a number if friendships, which are transient in nature. They are also egocentric, and less likely to see events from another child's perspective. Now is a perfect time to sow the seeds of how your child makes and develops friendships.

Older children usually have formed some close friendships, and have a definite preference for particular playmates. They are more socially aware, and difficulties with making (or falling out with) friends may surface around this time. Look for signs that your child can empathize with other children, and that he isn't misinterpreting verbal or non-verbal clues in other children's behaviour.

With all children, you should view the tests as an opportunity to discuss friendship, feelings and relationships. Boys tend to favour a group of friends, and interactions are more activity-based, like playing games or sport. Girls tend to have a close circle of friends, and perhaps one special friend, and interactions include talking about feelings.

Whiz**Kid**

Margaret Thatcher

Margaret Hilda Roberts was born in 1925 in Grantham, England. A clever child whose father was an ardent worker in local politics, she decided early in life to become a Member of Parliament. She studied chemistry at Oxford University, where she was the first woman president of the Oxford University Conservative Association. In 1959, she won a seat in Parliament. Analytical, articulate and ambitious, she soon become prominent among other politicians. In 1974 she became leader of the Conservative Party and then was elected prime minister – the first woman in Europe to achieve this.

Non-verbal communication

People-smart adults and children have a great understanding of how others are feeling, what they need or want and why they act the way they do. Key skills for understanding this are listening and observing. People give clues about how they really feel, or what they really want, in the way that they speak, and in their facial expressions and body movements. Someone with sensitivity will pick up on these.

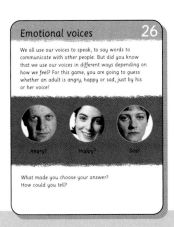

Emotional voices   26

We all use our voices to speak, to say words to communicate with other people. But did you know that we use our voices in different ways depending on how we feel? For this game, you are going to guess whether an adult is angry, happy or sad, just by his or her voice!

Angry?   Happy?   Sad?

What made you choose your answer?
How could you tell?

26 Emotional voices

Your child is going to try to identify emotions – which could be happiness, sadness, or anger – by your voice and your facial expression. Pick a well-known nursery rhyme or poem your child is familiar with and say it aloud to him, portraying different feelings – perhaps first sadness, then happiness and finally anger. Ask your child to say what he thinks you are – happy, sad or angry.

How did it go?

Did your child:
- Understand the activity?
- Enjoy guessing the emotions?
- Seem able to identify an emotion by the way you used your voice?

- Really get into the spirit of the activity?
- Demonstrate an increased interest in how people can use their voices or body language to convey emotion?

Boosting activities

- Watch a drama or film together on TV, and talk about what the characters might be feeling by the way they are speaking. See if your child can spot more subtle emotions, like anxiety, jealousy, surprise, fear or kindness.

- Sit down together with a pencil and paper and write down some words with similar meanings to happy, sad and angry. How about "cheerful" or "joyous" for happy, "glum" or "gloomy" for sad, or "furious" or "annoyed" for angry? This activity will improve your child's emotional vocabulary.

- Using a mirror, have your child practice facial expressions that match these sentences: "I don't understand", "I'm really glad to see you", "I didn't hear that", and "I'm really mad you broke my toy". Turn it into a game, and see if you can guess which sentence your child is showing you.

If the answer is "yes" to three or more of these questions, it reveals your child can sense emotion in voice and expressions, both crucial elements in being people smart. He is probably at ease in social situations that involve meeting new people.

If the answer is "no" to three or more of these questions, then your child may be new to the concept of emotion as an element of speech or body language. Explain to him how people shout and tense up when they are cross, or how a voice "lilts" and the person relaxes when she is happy.

Making and keeping friends

Friendships are a vital part of your child's life, and provide more than just playmates. Friendships help children develop emotionally and morally. They enable children to practice controlling their emotions and responding to the emotions of others. Through friendships, children learn how to communicate, cooperate, and solve problems. Friendships even affect school performance; children tend to have better attitudes about learning at school when they have friends there.

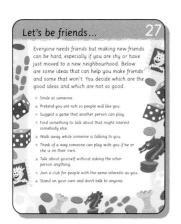

Let's be friends...   27

Everyone needs friends but making new friends can be hard, especially if you are shy or have just moved to a new neighbourhood. Below are some ideas that can help you make friends and some that won't. You decide which are the good ideas and which are not so good.

- Smile at someone.
- Pretend you are rich so people will like you.
- Suggest a game that another person can play.
- Find something to talk about that might interest somebody else.
- Walk away while someone is talking to you.
- Think of a way someone can play with you if he or she is on their own.
- Talk about yourself without asking the other person anything.
- Join a club for people with the same interests as you.
- Stand on your own and don't talk to anyone.

27 Let's be friends...

- You will need pencil and paper.

Set aside some time to talk through the "making friends" ideas with your child. Write "good ideas" and "not so good ideas" at the top of the paper, and place the ideas in the relevant column as your child decides. You should extend this activity by talking about her choices after the selection has been made. Ask your child why some ideas would work and some wouldn't, and why. Talk about any real-life examples of making friends.

Boosting activities

- Expand your child's circle of friends by inviting a child to play at your house. If your child is shy, arrange for a slightly younger child to visit so that your child gets a chance to lead. If your child is a bit bossy or has difficulty sharing, meet in a neutral place or take a picnic to the park.

- Have your child make a "social map". Write her name in the middle of a page, and ask her to add the names of the people she is closest to (friends and family) near it. Then add the names of acquaintances she isn't as close to further away. Encourage your child to add as many friends as possible. Talk about the map together – are there people she would like to get to know better?

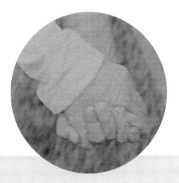

Correct answers

* **Stars** – good ideas
▲ **Triangles** – not so good ideas
Score 1 point for each correct answer

How did it go?

Six or more correct answers show that your child understands the fundamental "rules" about making friends and is well on the way to being people smart. These skills will be invaluable as she moves into adolescence and adulthood.

Five or less correct answers reveal that your child probably needs to reach out more to make friends. This takes courage because there is always the risk of rejection. Try to put a positive spin on any setbacks to boost your child's confidence, and talk about friendship on a regular basis.

Relationship challenges

There are times when even strong relationships are strained, and an important people-smart skill is the ability to resolve any differences by finding satisfying solutions. Young children often react to relationship problems in ineffective ways, like crying, hitting the other child or running to a parent or teacher. People-smart children approach problem-solving in a methodical way. Firstly, they work out what the problem is (a younger child hit me); secondly, they come up with some ideas for solving the problem (hit back, walk away, tell him not to hit) and thirdly, they evaluate each idea to come up with the best plan. Teaching problem-solving to children helps them to have happy, safe, and secure relationships.

What would you do if? 28

Do you ever argue with kids at school, or members of your family? Having disagreements isn't a bad thing in itself, but if you can't solve the issue it can really get you down.

Here are some difficult situations you might find yourself in. Think about all the different ways you might react. What's the best thing to do – and why?

▸ You and your brother or sister both want the last piece of pizza.

▸ You are playing with a toy and another child tries to take it from you.

▸ Your mother lets you wear her watch and you break it.

▸ You share something with a friend, but he or she refuses to give it back.

▸ Your teacher tells you off for something you didn't do.

28 What would you do if?

Set aside some time to talk through the scenarios on the card with your child. Make sure you are both relaxed and treat this activity more as a "chat" than a test. Evaluate whether your child (a) understands the problem, (b) can come up with some plans to resolve it, and (c) thinks about the consequences of acting in a particular way, so that he arrives at the best plan of action. Talk about the pros and cons of each "plan", and the consequences of putting that plan into action.

Boosting activities

■ Children learn the majority of their problem-solving skills from watching the adults in their lives interact. Include your child in any of the following family negotiations: which TV programme to watch, where to go on Saturday, who should clear the table, what to cook for supper, or whose turn it is to have a friend to play.

■ Problem-solving is helped by the ability to see the other person's perspective and anticipate his or her emotions – this is called empathy. You can promote empathy in your kids by encouraging them to volunteer their time to help others.

How did it go?

Did your child:
■ Understand the activity?
■ Enjoy discussing the various scenarios?
■ Seem able to come up with ideas for problem-solving and conflict resolutions, and evaluate them thoughtfully?
■ Really get into the spirit of the activity?
■ Demonstrate an increased awareness of problem-solving or conflict resolution after the activity?

If the answer is "yes" to three or more of these questions, it reveals that your child is likely to be good at resolving conflicts, which is useful both in forming lasting friendships and in acting as a negotiator with peers.

If the answer is "no" to three or more of these questions, then your child may be relying on immature methods of problem-solving, and he just needs to learn some alternatives that are more likely to bring a permanent peace.

Social setbacks

We've all had times when we have felt rejected or tried to join a conversation and have been met with a frosty reception. Children experience this, too. Some children react angrily, and feel others are mean or "out to get them", while other children withdraw and think they just aren't fun to be around. People-smart kids tend to view rejections as temporary or think they could have done something differently to improve the outcome. They recognize that the situation itself might have led to the rejection – if two children play with a truck each, they could find it difficult to include another in the game. The parents of people-smart children have helped their kids see that social situations can be improved with effort and positive behaviour, and these children have an optimistic view of others and themselves as friends.

Why do things go wrong?

Making friends isn't always easy. You may have asked a classmate to come over and play and he or she said "Sorry, I can't." You probably felt hurt, but there might have been a good reason why he or she couldn't come. For example, your classmate might have been busy on that day, or might have felt sad because he or she had a bad day at school, or you might not have smiled or seemed very friendly. What do you think may be behind the following situations:

▶ You ask if you can eat lunch with a group of children at school, and they say "No."

▶ You see two friends talking together, but when you join them the conversation stops.

▶ You normally sit next to your next-door neighbour on the school bus, but this morning he or she was sitting with someone else.

29 Why do things go wrong?

Set aside some time to talk through the scenarios on the card with your child. Make sure you are both relaxed and pick an informal location, so that your child feels you are having a conversation rather than being assessed. Look out for suggestions that are both external (to do with the other child) and internal (to do with your child). You can extend the activity by talking about how your child might do things differently in each of the scenarios.

Boosting activities

■ To encourage your child to see the good in everyone, make a family "praise box" from an old shoe box, decorating it together. Put it with pen and paper in a prominent place in your home. Encourage all family members to praise each other for something specific by writing a short note, and placing it in the box. Open the box once a week and take turns reading the notes.

■ Read the children's story *Pollyanna*, by Eleanor H. Porter. Pollyanna plays the "glad game", which is about finding a silver lining in every cloud, and she transforms the lives of those around her. See if you can play the "glad game" in your family!

How did it go?

Did your child:
■ Understand the activity?
■ Seem able to relate to the various scenarios?
■ Seem able to suggest both external and internal reasons for the other children's behaviour?
■ Really get into the spirit of the activity?
■ Demonstrate an increased ability to see social setbacks in a positive light?

If the answer is "yes" to three or more of these questions, your child is definitely people smart, and is emotionally resilient and optimistic. She will find relationships easy and rewarding in adult life.

If the answer is "no" to three or more of these questions, your child is probably too young at present to see the other person's side; this comes with maturity and age. Provide optimistic suggestions for social setbacks, to encourage your child to open up to new people.

What is Self**Smart**?

People who know themselves well and have a strong sense of who they are, their strengths and weaknesses, are self smart. These people think about, and learn from, past experiences. Developing this type of intelligence reinforces confidence, self-control, and assertiveness which lead to happy, stable relationships and success in life.

While it could be argued that it doesn't matter too much if someone doesn't exploit musical or artistic ability, understanding our emotional motivations is essential for every aspect of our lives. At the core of personal intelligence is the ability to think about and distinguish between feelings, recognize them as discrete emotions, and then use them to direct behaviour. This chapter includes tests on three aspects of self smart, each addressing a key area:

- Who am I? – an examination of temperament, the in-built aspect of character and personality.
- Being myself – recognizing and taking ownership of feelings.
- I can choose – the difference between feelings and reactions, and choosing how and when to act on emotions.

Encouraging personal intelligence

Being self smart is your child's greatest key to success. When your child has completed the tests, you will both have a better idea of what she is good at, and what she finds difficult. A great way of improving self smart is to help your child set goals. Goals can be big ("I want to be Prime Minister!") or small ("I want to finish reading my book"). They can be for things you want to do today ("I want to spend some time drawing") or in the future ("I want to learn to play the guitar"). The key thing is that they are for specific things your child really cares about, and are realistic but challenging. Have your child set goals and review them regularly.

Emotional intelligence, which includes self smart, is learned from your child's home environment. Your child watches how you manage your own emotions, and how you react to situations. You also may be inadvertently teaching your child how to deal with her feelings by how you coach her in expressing her emotions. Do you believe that girls shouldn't be "pushy" or that boys shouldn't cry?

Helping your child with the activities

The activities are best done in sequence, because each one builds on knowledge gained from the previous one. An understanding of temperament can be viewed as the foundation stone. This is followed by the recognition of feelings and learning to distinguish between them. Finally, once your child understands her feelings, she can begin to control them and think before acting on them.

The nature of the tests calls for your child to reveal personal information about herself. There are no right or wrong answers. You must respect your child's right to withhold things from you, or to discontinue the tests if she feels uncomfortable. Children need to feel that they are not being judged, or punished for giving a "wrong" answer. It is possible that while doing a test your child may tell you something you weren't expecting or find upsetting. In this case, discontinue the test, and use the opportunity to gently question her about it. Don't panic; take time out to consider the best course of action.

What to look for

Younger children may need some time to understand the tests, so make sure you talk through the ideas behind each one before you start. Their responses may be a bit immature, because they are still learning about their feelings and how to deal with them. You could use the subject matter simply as a springboard for talking about feelings together as a family.

Older children are more likely to feel inhibited about discussing their feelings with you, so you need to make sure you are non-judgmental and non-threatening. Talk about your own feelings openly to create a climate of trust. 7-9-year-olds will have more self-knowledge through attending school, and will know their scholastic strengths and weaknesses. Explain that their personal development is just the same.

Whiz**Kid**

Harry Houdini

Born in Budapest, Hungary in 1874, Erik Weisz ran away from home when he was just 12 in order to earn money and seek adventure. He travelled around the country for about a year and then met his father in New York City. He was very athletic and won awards in swimming and track, building up the stamina and strength he needed to succeed as an escape artist. Houdini's formal education was limited, but his self-education was immense. He was often quoted as saying "My mind is the key that sets me free."

Personality types

Everyone has natural inborn traits, which we call "temperament". Our temperament consists of attitudes, moods and inclinations, which affect how character and personality develop through childhood. Carl Jung, the Swiss psychologist, proposed four main types of temperament based on how people make decisions: sensing (using information from your five senses), intuitive (listening to your inner voice), thinking (making decisions based on logic) and feeling (making decisions based on emotions).

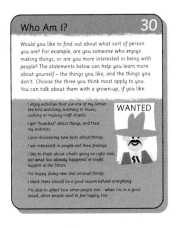

Who Am I? 30

Would you like to find out about what sort of person you are? For example, are you someone who enjoys making things, or are you more interested in being with people? The statements below can help you learn more about yourself – the things you like, and the things you don't. Choose the three you think most apply to you. You can talk about them with a grown-up, if you like.

I enjoy activities that use one of my senses like bird-watching, listening to music, cooking or making craft objects.

I get "hunches" about things, and trust my instincts.

I love discovering new facts about things.

I am interested in people and their feelings.

I like to think about what's going on right now, not what has already happened or might happen in the future.

I'm happy doing new and unusual things.

I think there should be a good reason behind everything.

I'm able to affect how other people feel – when I'm in a good mood, other people start to feel happy, too.

WANTED

30 Who am I?

Most children are a blend of the four personality types but will have one that is dominant. Helping children discover their temperament type enables them to learn about themselves emotionally. Self-smart children and adults are aware of their temperament, and can play to its strengths and overcome its weaknesses.

Begin by introducing the idea of temperament and personality – that everyone has a natural inclination towards certain ways of thinking and behaving. Older children may want some privacy while reading through the test, but, with younger children, you may need to talk about each statement so that you are sure they understand what it means. You can extend the activity by choosing statements that apply to you, and discussing your temperament with your child.

Boosting activities

- Talk about how someone from each temperament might feel or act differently. What sort of hobbies might they have? What sort of jobs might they do? An intuitive person might make a good counsellor; a sensing person might enjoy playing a musical instrument, for example.

- Have your child draw up a list of any decisions he has made today or in the past week (like who he played with, and TV programmes he watched). What influenced those decisions, why did he act in the way he did? Think about the decisions in the light of your child's temperament type.

How did it go?

Choosing the first and fifth statements indicates a "sensing" temperament. Your child depends on his senses, and is adaptable, practical and realistic. The weakness of a sensing temperament is a tendency to live in the present, without learning from the past or anticipating the future.

Choosing the second and sixth statements indicates an "intuitive" temperament. Your child has a strong inner voice, and can detect patterns in information or behaviour. The weakness of an intuitive temperament is a tendency to worry more about the future than the present, and a dislike of routine.

Choosing the third and seventh statements indicates a "thinking" temperament. Your child has a strong sense of logic, and uses his intellect to evaluate things rationally. The weakness of a thinking temperament is a tendency to seem cold and unemotional, and a difficulty in talking about feelings.

Choosing the fourth and eighth statements indicates a "feeling" temperament. Your child is emotionally warm and has a strong sense of ethics, and of what is "good" and "bad". The weakness of a feeling temperament is a tendency to be emotionally manipulative and to be "touchy" or take things the wrong way.

If your child's three choices are from three different temperament types, your child has a blend of temperaments.

Understanding emotions

We all experience a wide range of emotions daily. Some are rare, some occur regularly. A key element of being self smart is the ability to recognize the feelings that can spring up inside us. Understanding emotions can help us express them, and once you know how you feel, you can start to understand why. This emotional insight is an ability self-smart people use every day in their dealings with others. Children often lack the emotional vocabulary to pinpoint uncomfortable feelings, which can lead to inappropriate reactions. But being able to name a feeling can help them handle it.

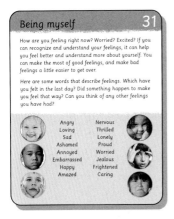

Being myself   **31**

How are you feeling right now? Worried? Excited? If you can recognize and understand your feelings, it can help you feel better and understand more about yourself. You can make the most of good feelings, and make bad feelings a little easier to get over.

Here are some words that describe feelings. Which have you felt in the last day? Did something happen to make you feel that way? Can you think of any other feelings you have had?

Angry
Loving
Sad
Ashamed
Annoyed
Embarrassed
Happy
Amazed

Nervous
Thrilled
Lonely
Proud
Worried
Jealous
Frightened
Caring

31 Being myself

Introduce the idea of emotions – that everyone has a range of feelings, which aren't right or wrong, or good or bad, and that they change. For younger children, talk about the meaning of each word and give examples, if necessary. You also could describe the physical sensations that go with some of these emotions – when you're angry you feel tense or hot, and when you're anxious you have butterflies in your tummy. Older children may want some privacy while reading through the activity. These tests require your child to reveal personal information to you and you should remember that it is a privilege and not something that you should demand. You can extend the activity by taking part and discussing your feelings with your child.

Boosting activities

■ Help your child make a "comfort box" for times when she feels sad and needs an emotional lift. Fill it with items that evoke good memories or are uplifting for your child – a holiday photo, a favourite music tape, a sports medal, an old cuddly toy, some of her favourite sweets, or a recipe for hot chocolate you can make together. Store the box until needed.

■ Let your child choose one of the emotions (positive or negative) that she identified and linked with a particular incident. Talk about the actual events. Discuss what your child thought and felt. Ask questions like, "What happened then?", "What did you think?", "How did that make you feel?" and "How do you feel about it now?".

How did it go?

Did your child:
■ Understand the activity?
■ Seem able to identify the emotions she experienced?
■ Identify any other emotions not listed?
■ Really get into the spirit of the activity?
■ Demonstrate an increased awareness of her emotional range after the activity?

If the answer is "yes" to three or more of these question, it indicates that your child has good self-awareness, since identifying emotions is the first step in managing them. Self-smart people regularly think about how they are feeling, and use this insight to cope with difficult emotions.

If the answer is "no" to three or more of these questions, then it may be because your child is younger, and her emotional vocabulary will be more limited. Talk about what each of the words mean, and give examples that are relevant to your child.

Dealing with emotions

One of the skills self-smart people have is the ability to separate thoughts, feelings and reactions. This is hard to do, because in reality they often occur almost simultaneously – you are shouted at, you feel hurt, you shout back. It can be helpful to distinguish between these steps – thoughts are a cognitive process, feelings are a psychological outcome and reactions are the physical response. The advantage of stopping yourself from acting before you have thought things through and examined your feelings is that you can plan the most effective response, and it usually isn't the first reaction that comes to mind.

32 I can choose

Read through each statement with your child and let her decide whether A and B are feelings or actions.

A great way of teaching your child about the difference is to use a traffic-light analogy. When something happens, think of it as a red light, and stop and think about what the problem is. The "light" will change to amber, so you pause to put a name to your feelings and plan the best course of action. When you are ready with your plan, then it's green for go.

While talking through the "traffic light" with your child, emphasize the difference between a feeling (in your head) and an action (what you actually do). Extend this activity by talking about other possible actions and whether they would be good or bad choices.

Boosting activities

■ Practice relaxation techniques with your child by tensing different muscles and then relaxing them. You could lie on the floor together and tense your whole bodies – then let go and feel yourselves melt into the floor. Teach your child that relaxing with a deep breath buys time to think and will calm her nerves.

■ Role play is a very successful technique for helping children deal with difficult situations, particularly those that crop up regularly. Discuss with your child what those situations are, and then re-enact them as you "play" the other child. This will help your child prepare for difficult events and practice saying uncomfortable things.

How did it go?

If your child got five or more correct answers it reveals she is able to make the distinction between feelings and actions, a key element of being self smart. Reinforce this ability by asking about actions and feelings in real life – it's much harder to stop and think in the heat of the moment.

Four or less correct answers show your child may need more coaching from you in the difference between feelings and actions. Talk over the statements on the card, and explain that what you think or feel about something is different from what you do about it.

Correct answers

Score 1 point for each correct answer

1A **feeling** ▪ 1B **action**

2A **action** ▪ 2B **feeling**

3A **feeling** ▪ 3B **action**

4A **action** ▪ 4B **feeling**

5A **feeling** ▪ 5B **action**

What is Nature**Smart**?

Naturalistic intelligence is the ability to nurture, identify and classify plants, animals, and natural phenomena. We all know people who are "green-fingered" and can grow and nurture plants, or those who have an incredible empathy with animals.

Children who are nature smart love being outdoors; they enjoy keeping pets, growing plants from seed, collecting fossils, reading nature books or watching TV shows on the natural world. They usually have an interest in "exciting" species like dinosaurs or sharks.

There are two nature-smart tests in this book and they cover the two most important skills associated with naturalistic intelligence:

- Observation – the ability to notice and interpret subtle changes in nature.
- Classification – the ability to sort and classify natural objects by distinguishing between features.

Encouraging natural intelligence at home
Developing nature smart has a positive impact on other intelligences, too. Sorting a collection of feathers or rocks calls on thinking smart. Nurturing a pet or plant helps self smart.

Working out the relationships between people, plants and animals in an ecosystem involves people smart. As many natural activities are done outdoors, there also are the physical and emotional health benefits of being out and at one with nature. So encouraging your child's nature smart will help her grow as a person.

If you live near countryside, or in a rural area, you probably already take advantage of the great outdoors. It takes more planning and effort to get in touch with nature if you live in an urban environment. If you don't have a garden you can still keep a window box of flowers or herbs, or a few fish in a tank. Small mammals such as hamsters can live in a cage in a child's room. Try to visit parks or nature reserves in your free time, and take advantage of the knowledgeable guides who work there. Most cities have zoos, where you can see and learn about animals close up.

Helping your child with the activities
Keep in mind the purpose of the activity as you undertake it with your child: powers of observation or the ability to sort and classify. Overlook any other aspect, such as impatience, disorganization, or messiness! You are looking for a real love of nature, and an enthusiasm for things in the natural world.

The nature-smart tests are quite time-intensive – we have to slow to nature's pace – so you won't get a quick answer about your child's abilities. It's best to plan these activities for a weekend, or in the school holidays, when you have plenty of time available. These are great projects for you to do together or even as a family; you may learn something yourself!

What to look for

Children aged 4–6 may just not have the patience or concentration to stick with the tests; they tend to like quick results and to move swiftly onto the next thing that fires their enthusiasm. Do spend time doing the activities together, because a young child is more likely to stick at something if she is receiving your full attention. Children are naturally curious, though, so keep things fresh and exciting by pointing out features they might miss.

Older children love the freedom that the outdoors and nature offers them, and are likely to respond well to both tests. They should be able to remain attentive to longer tasks, so lack of concentration is less of an issue. You may find distraction is more the problem, so perhaps combine the activities with a bike ride, or a picnic lunch and make a day of it."

Whiz**Kid**

Charles Darwin

Darwin was born in Shropshire, England in 1809. Even as a boy Darwin loved science and his enthusiasm for chemical studies earned him the name "Gas" from his friends. He was also an avid collector of anything "natural", which demonstrates his flair for nature smart.

In 1831, aged 22, he joined the survey ship, *HMS Beagle* as its naturalist. The round-the-world journey lasted almost five years, and throughout the journey, Darwin shipped back crate loads of tropical plants, insects, shells and fossil animals. On his return, Darwin studied his collections and notes from the voyage, and hit upon the idea of Natural Selection, the most widely accepted theory on evolution today.

Observing nature

Although nature smart can be difficult to tune into if you live in an urban environment, we all take notice of the weather, so it's a great way to encourage a key nature-smart skill – observation.

Weather watch   **33**

You can learn a great deal about nature by keeping track of the weather. If you note down your daily weather, you'll start to see patterns, and you might be able to make predictions, like a real weather forecaster!

Every day for at least two weeks, write an entry in your "weather diary", a small notebook used for the purpose. Use a thermometer to measure temperature and a measuring jug to capture rainfall. You could include all or any of these ideas in your diary:

- The maximum temperature during the day.
- The minimum temperature at night.
- The daily rainfall amount.
- Is it sunny or cloudy? What do the clouds look like?
- Is it windy? What direction is the wind coming from?

Can you see any relationships between different aspects of weather or unusual changes in the weather? You could compare your actual weather with a real weather forecast on the TV, Internet or in the newspaper.

33 Weather watch

- You will need a small notebook, a minimum/maximum temperature thermometer and a small measuring jug for catching rainfall.

To assess your child's powers of observation in the natural world, help him write a weather diary. It can be as simple or as complicated as he wants – although it might be better to start with just a couple of measurements if you think your child might get bored with record-keeping. You could extend this activity by asking him to find out more about clouds – how they are formed and what the different formations mean.

Boosting activities

■ Take up stargazing. Buy or borrow a
book or star chart that shows the
major constellations. Dress warmly, and
lie on the ground together on a blanket.
Using a flashlight to read the book or
chart, see how many star groups you
can find. Most children don't know
that the signs of the zodiac can be
found in the sky!

■ Watch television nature programmes
together and talk about what you see.
Try National Geographic or the
Discovery Channel.

How did it go?

Did your child:
■ Understand the activities?
■ Enjoy taking weather measurements?
■ Seem able to take weather
measurements and interpret findings
with ease?
■ Really get into the spirit of the activities?
■ Demonstrate an increased interest in
observing the weather?

If the answer is "yes" to three or more of
these questions, then your child has excellent
observation and classifying skills, which are
fundamental to being nature smart. Build on
these skills by observing nature and
classifying other natural materials, like leaves
or shells, together.

If the answer is "no" to three or more of
these questions, then it could be because
your child is younger, and you may need to
build up your child's concentration by finding
out what fires his enthusiasm.

Classifying nature

There is so much going on around us in the natural world. If you look in just one corner of your garden, or a flower bed in the park, you'll see several plant species growing alongside one another, insects crawling on the ground or flying through the air, or spiders weaving their webs among the leaves. These situations may appear to be chaotic, but they are, in fact, highly ordered, both in the natural way plants and animals live and grow, and in terms of the way scientists describe and classify living things. The ability to classify, to bring order and sense to an environmental situation, is another attribute of nature smart, and one that draws on thinking smart, too.

What's that tree?   34

Outside, all around you, are lots of different types, or species, of trees. You probably know the names of some trees, but did you know you can find out the name of any tree by studying a leaf and looking at how it grows?

1 Collect a number of different tree leaves. Notice the way the leaves grow on the tree – are they exactly opposite one another, or are they staggered, alternating on each side of the twig? Make a drawing to show the way the leaves are growing and the pattern of the veins in the leaf. You could even take a photo of the tree.

2 Using your samples and notes, look up your leaf in a reference book or on the Internet (ask a grown-up to help you with this).

3 Fix your leaf, photograph (if you have one) and your drawing to a scrapbook, and label your samples.

4 Keep adding to your collection until you have classified ten or more trees.

34   What's that tree?

- You will need a reference book on leaves or Internet access, a scrapbook for storing specimens, glue for fixing specimens, a pen and a camera (optional).

Your child will create a collection of tree leaves and, with your help, identify and label each specimen. You can find tree-identification sites on the Internet or you can buy or borrow a reference book – try the gardening section of your bookstore or library. You could extend this activity by researching families of trees (types of trees grouped together because they are similar), or by making leaf rubbings (by placing the leaf under tracing paper and rubbing a crayon over the surface).

Boosting activities

- Plan a visit to a natural history museum, zoo, or aquarium, and explore the different methods for classifying plants and animals that scientists use. Do you think they make sense? Can you think of other ways?

- Plant a tree at your school, park, or in your garden. Many areas have tree-planting programmes in the spring or autumn.

How did it go?

Did you child:

- Understand the activity?
- Enjoy collecting leaf samples?
- Seem able to notice slight differences in leaf formation?
- Really get into the spirit of the activity?
- Demonstrate an increased interest in collecting and classifying natural objects?

If the answer is "yes" to three or more of these questions, then your child has excellent observation and classifying skills, which are fundamental to being nature smart. Build on these skills by observing nature and classifying other natural materials, like leaves and shells, together.

If the answer is "no" to three or more of these questions, then it could be because your child is younger, and you may need to build up your child's concentration by finding out what fires his enthusiasm.

Index

Acknowledgments

The author would like to thank:

Dr Kirsty Smedley, Consultant Clinical Psychologist, for her expertise and advice, and for being my sister.
My husband Chris, for supporting and encouraging me.
My daughter Beth, for the fun we have.
The other children in my life ... Abby, Ben, Callum, George, Harry Joe, Jordan and Ruby.
And finally, the dedicated and talented team at Carroll & Brown, especially Amy Carroll and Denise Brown.

Carroll & Brown would like to thank:

Production Karol Davies
IT Management Paul Stradling

Date	Card	Results/Remarks

Date	Card	Results/Remarks

Date	Card	Results/Remarks

Date	Card	Results/Remarks

Date	Card	Results/Remarks

Date	Card	Results/Remarks

Date	Card	Results/Remarks

Date	Card	Results/Remarks

Date	Card	Results/Remarks

Date	Card	Results/Remarks

Date	Card	Results/Remarks

Date	Card	Results/Remarks

Date	Card	Results/Remarks

Date	Card	Results/Remarks

Date	Card	Results/Remarks

Date	Card	Results/Remarks